FRESH VEGGIE BBQ

First published in the United Kingdom in 2019 by
Pavilion
43 Great Ormond Street
London
WC1N 3HZ

ISBN 978-1-91162-465-3

A CIP catalogue record for this book is available from the
British Library.

10 9 8 7 6 5 4 3 2 1

Reproduction by Mission Productions Ltd, Hong Kong
Printed and bound by Toppan Leefung Printing Ltd, China

www.pavilionbooks.com

FRESH VEGGIE BBQ

ALL NATURAL & DELICIOUS RECIPES FROM THE GRILL

DAVID & CHARLOTTE BAILEY

PAVILION

CONTENTS

INTRODUCTION

Just 10 years ago, when we first fell in love with a Citroën H van and ended up starting our vegetarian street food business, we could never have predicted the extraordinary explosion of plant-based eating that was to come. While we've always done fairly well, back in the early days we lost count of the number of people who thought we were very stupid to have an exclusively vegetarian truck, and time and time again we were asked if we'd ever considered 'putting chicken in it' or thought about having a 'meat alternative too'. Happily, things have changed beyond recognition and now we can hardly keep up with how many veggie and vegan openings there are, and we hardly ever encounter somebody with a resistance to trying something 'because it's vegetarian'.

In the shops, too, a revolution has occurred. Where we once spent hours making our own 'mylks' and experimenting with vegan cheeses or making our own meat substitutes, the shops are now full to the brim with numerous varieties of tiger nut milk and a seemingly endless array of seitan, soya or jackfruit products. There are even vegetarian 'butchers' these days. It's wonderful!

But one area where meat still seems to dominate, and the vegetarians and vegans get a bit overlooked, is at the barbecue. And it's such a shame. We love barbecues, we love fire, we love being outdoors, we agree that nothing beats that smoky taste only barbecuing can achieve. And while we do love veggie burgers and we aren't quite sick to death of halloumi just yet, the world of veggie barbecues definitely needs some fresh ideas!

As mobile caterers usually to be found 'in the field', as the very proud tenants of a glorious allotment, and with Dave being a very keen outdoorsman who despite nearly 25 years of London living constantly yearns to recreate the open spaces and outdoor lifestyle of his South African upbringing, this has been the perfect mission for us; one that has pulled together all of our most favourite things and we really hope you enjoy what we've come up with in this, our third recipe book.

Essentially, there are two main ways to enjoy cooking outdoors. The first is the more elemental – cooking on the fire pit with wood – and the second is on the barbecue using charcoal (we always use natural lumpwood).

WOOD

There is something so raw and primal about fire, and there is little that creates as much atmosphere, that's as satisfying and that amplifies flavour so much as harnessing its power for cooking. The simplicity, smell and smoky woody flavour that results from this way of cooking really can't be beaten and we love to prepare meals at the fire pit at our allotment, or when we're away camping, but there are a few little challenges and limitations. The first is that you do need the space, and the second is that you do also tend to need quite a lot of wood as it doesn't generally last as long as charcoal, although some companies (like London Log Company, for example) sell engineered logs that are very long lasting.

But if you're going to go for it (which we highly recommend), to build a wood fire you're first going to need something to contain it and to protect it from the weather. This will usually be some form of fire pit made from something like a large ring of stones or a metal drum or fire ring. A similar set-up will also be needed to support a grill grate, if using.

Another straightforward way, more akin to a normal barbecue, is to track down a portable log-burning stove. The Frontier Stove from Netherton Foundry is a favourite of ours.

RECIPE KEY

V = Vegan
VO = Vegan Option
WF = Wheat-free
GF = Gluten-free

To build the fire, we usually start with firelighters (we try to always use eco ones) and some kindling. When that's caught, we top it with some larger twigs and branches and when that's nicely burning too, we add the logs over the flame in a large tepee formation.

At this point, the fire will hopefully begin to blaze, and while you don't usually use that stage to cook, it is possible to work with some of the Dutch oven dishes using a tripod. Generally though, you wait for about 20 minutes until it's burned down to a bed of coals (embers) that are perfect for cooking over. This should be enough for most dishes but if you're doing a recipe that needs to cook for a long time, you may need to add more logs.

We'd only recommend using hardwoods such as beech, oak, birch or sweet chestnut, as softer woods like pine are trickier to light and also contain resins that interfere with the flavour of the food. Again, the London Log Company is a great source of suitable woods and firelighters, as well as lumpwood charcoals if you're going that way instead, and all kinds of other useful things.

CHARCOAL

While we do love to use a live fire and are lucky enough to have the space at our allotment to regularly do so, there are certainly advantages to a charcoal set-up and we do, fairly frequently, turn to our Weber.

Firstly, it's definitely easier and less bulky to get hold of lumpwood charcoal than it is wood, but secondly, it is also somewhat easier to control than the raging flames of a wood fire. Another plus is that the embers last much longer and you do also always have the option of recreating some of the extraordinary flavours of the live fire by soaking wood chips (we love to use oak, hickory, mesquite and maple) and then scattering them over your hot coals.

To get a barbecue going in this way, we generally place a couple of firelighters into the kettle, a good distance apart from each other. Then, with a pair of tongs, we put plenty of charcoal around each one but leaving room between them for air to circulate. We ignite the firelighters and then leave it for about 5 minutes while they in turn ignite the charcoal. When they're ignited too, we add more charcoal and then leave that to burn for about 20–30 minutes. If you've got a lid, make sure the air vents are left open. It's ready when there's no more open flame and the coals are all glowing red.

Patience is king with this and a lot of issues arise from not waiting for the coals to be hot enough or not putting enough on. But if patience is an issue (we're talking about ourselves here), we highly recommend getting hold of a chimney starter. This cheap bit of kit makes life so much easier and you'll have a load of burning coals ready before you even know it.

Whichever way you go, we've divided this book for ease into outdoor cooking techniques that can work either way: Dutch oven, skillet/chapa, grill/parrilla and embers and ashes, before moving on to things to prepare in advance or that are non-cook, such as salads, marinades, sauces, pickles, sides and drinks.

Here is an explanation and our top tips for each technique:

DUTCH OVEN/CAULDRON

The big cast iron pot is steeped in history and most traditions have one, from the *potjie* of Africa to the *calderos* of the Argentinian pampas. And the sight of one is emotive, conjuring up images of great wilderness explorers stopping for sustenance under vast starry skies.

It's possible to cook up stews on an open fire by erecting a tripod around the flames then carefully hanging the Dutch oven slightly offset from the main flame so it's more safe in the event of overboiling. Alternatively, it can be placed directly in the embers (and you can use a charcoal shovel to build embers up around it and on top of it if the recipe calls for that). Or, if you're using a barbecue, just remove the grate so you can place it directly on the coals.

Make sure you have something like a tent peg and a barbecue glove to hand so you can safely lift the lid to check progress. Use double the amount of coals on the top of the pot as to the bottom, so it doesn't get too hot underneath, and remember to move the coals from the bottom to the top if you suspect it's too hot underneath. Steam is a telltale sign.

If you're indoors, you can just use the hob (stove) and oven.

SKILLET/CHAPA

Chapa is a Spanish word that simply translates as 'flat piece of metal'. And that's really all it is: a piece of flat cast iron set over a fire. Many chapas are like fire tables and come with legs, but you can alternatively use bricks to prop the sheet up. They are a wonderful bit of kit, but the alternative, which we have tended to work with in these recipes, is to just use a cast iron skillet or flat griddle plate/pan, placed over the barbecue grate. This is also the way to adapt most of these recipes for home – you can use a skillet or griddle plate when cooking indoors on the hob.

GRILL/PARRILLA

This refers to any cast iron barbecue grate, from the famous Latin American *parrilla* to the grate that comes with a Weber. If you're cooking on open fire without a frame, this is where you'll need some stones or fireproof bricks to support it.

EMBERS & ASHES

Commonly known as *rescoldo*, this is a cooking technique that buries its ingredients in hot embers and ashes. It's especially suitable for cooking vegetables and is a way to use up every part of the fire, even the dying embers. Whatever you cook in this way will get a blackened skin that, when later removed, reveals an incredible depth of burned, charred flavour.

FAVOURITE EQUIPMENT

Cast iron stuff – completely fireproof and utterly indestructible, although one of Dave's earliest camping memories is of making dinner in a cast iron potjie pot in the South African bush and waking the next morning to find the handle had been chewed by a hyena! Unlikely to be a problem closer to home, cast iron is still our number one choice for a Dutch oven and skillet. Ours are both by Lodge.

If you're going for open-fire cooking, you might also want to think about a chapa, which provides a flat surface, and a parrilla, which is a barbecue grate. Netherton Foundry is a great source (and for cast iron items in general), but Sizzle Grills also do very nice ones.

- **Heavy-duty barbecue tongs** – we generally find the longer the better.

- **Heavy-duty gloves** – we usually buy welding gloves for this purpose.

- **Grill brush** – keep your grate clean!

- **Coal shovel** – for moving around the embers; very useful in the embers-and-ashes dishes and those recipes in the Dutch oven section that need to 'bake' and so need the embers piled around them.

- **A tent peg** – very handy for lifting the Dutch oven lid!

- **Metal spatula** – the key to successful flipping.

- **Bricks** – vital for resting anything super hot on. They are also very useful for propping up a barbecue grate or a chapa/skillet and can be used either standing up or flat to be further away or closer to the coals.

- **Griddle plate** – for bringing the barbecue party indoors. Look again to Lodge who do a reversible one that can be used outdoors but also turns your hob into an excellent grill!

- **Chimney starter** – Perfect when you want your coals hot quick!

- **A strong apron** – Dave tends to model the one from Labour and Wait. Just make sure it's protective and, of course, chic.

- **Axe** – Dave loves his Gransfors Bruks axe. It's good to have one around to feel like the real McCoy but also to split logs and to chop up sticks and branches for kindling.

We've had an awful lot of fun creating this book and really believe that fun is the secret ingredient in making good food, especially at a barbecue! Cooking generally – but particularly when you throw into the mix the great outdoors and the element of fire – is never an exact science, but it is certainly one that is always elevated by having a good time, breaking rules, improvising, experimenting and trusting your intuition. We really hope this book encourages you to enjoy more time outdoors, with friends and family, relaxing, having lots of laughs and gorging on great food.

A final word of warning: if you're going to be making any of these dishes at not exclusively vegetarian barbecues, do make sure the meat eaters don't steal all your efforts! It seems to be a commonly experienced phenomenon.

DUTCH OVEN

BLACK BEAN & FIRE-ROASTED TOMATO JAMBALAYA

SERVES 2–4
VO / WF / GF

Arguably the cornerstone of New Orleans cuisine, jambalaya was the result of the Spanish inhabitants of the New World trying to recreate their beloved paella. The impossible-to-source saffron was replaced with tomatoes and as time went on French and then Caribbean influences came in. It's a super one-pot dish, ideal after an active day spent in the great outdoors. We tend to use VegiDeli or Cauldron sausages, but any that you enjoy will be perfect.

400g/14oz fresh plum tomatoes
200g/7oz vegetarian sausages
1 tbsp vegetable oil
1 onion, chopped
2 garlic cloves, crushed
1 red pepper, diced
3 sticks celery, diced
2 tsp dried oregano
1 tsp smoked paprika
½ tsp cayenne pepper
2 bay leaves
200g/7oz/1 cup short-grain brown rice, uncooked
500ml/17fl oz/2 cups vegetable stock
500ml/17fl oz/2 cups water
1 x 400-g/14-oz can black beans, drained and rinsed
10g/⅓oz parsley, chopped
salt (optional) and black pepper
sliced jalapeño chillies, to serve
sour cream, to serve

If you're cooking outdoors, begin by placing the whole tomatoes and the sausages on the grill and allow them to char on both sides. Remove from the grill and when cool enough to handle, roughly chop the tomatoes and slice the sausages, then leave to one side. This will give them a lovely smoky flavour, but it's not vital if you're cooking on the hob (stove) indoors. If that's the case, just roughly chop the tomatoes and slice the sausages without any initial cooking and also leave to one side.

Place your Dutch oven over your chosen heat source and heat the vegetable oil over a medium heat. Add the onion and sauté for a couple of minutes before adding the garlic, red pepper and celery. Continue to sauté for about 10 minutes, stirring occasionally. Add the oregano, smoked paprika, cayenne pepper and bay leaves and cook for a minute or two before stirring in the chopped tomatoes. Stir in the rice and then add the vegetable stock, water and a little black pepper. Cover with a lid and leave to simmer for about 15 minutes. Add the beans and sliced sausages, cover again and continue to cook for another 40 minutes, stirring regularly and checking often that it's not catching. If it is catching, or looks too thick at any point, just add a little more water as needed.

It's ready when the rice is cooked. Remove from the heat and leave to one side for another 10 minutes to let the flavours infuse. Season to taste, remove the bay leaves and stir through the parsley. Serve with jalapeño slices and sour cream on the side.

Vegan option Use vegan sausages and omit the sour cream.

For the shortcrust pastry

225g/8oz/1¾ cups plain (all-purpose) flour (use wholemeal if you prefer), plus extra for dusting

100g/3½oz/scant ½ cup cold butter, diced

pinch of salt

1 egg, whisked, for brushing

For the filling

3 tbsp olive oil

1 onion, chopped

2 garlic cloves, crushed

80g/2¾oz leek, chopped

10 sprigs thyme, picked and roughly chopped

250g/9oz wild mushrooms, cleaned

salt and black pepper

1 x 400-g/14-oz can artichoke hearts, drained and quartered

125ml/4fl oz/½ cup white wine or beer (optional)

300ml/10½fl oz/1¼ cups single (light) cream

20g/¾oz parsley, roughly chopped

WILD MUSHROOM & ARTICHOKE ONE-POT PIE

SERVES 4

This is a good one for autumn evenings that are too lovely to stay indoors. Shortcrust pastry is very easy to make, but you can of course use shop-bought if you prefer. Wild mushrooms are always our preference but you can use quartered brown mushrooms if they're unavailable.

Begin by making the shortcrust pastry. Sift the flour into a large bowl and then rub in the butter with your fingertips until the mixture resembles breadcrumbs. Add the salt along with 2–3 tablespoons of water and mix with your hands to form a firm dough. Turn the dough out onto a floured surface and gently knead for a minute or so before wrapping in clingfilm (plastic wrap) and transferring to the fridge or a cool spot to chill.

If you're cooking indoors, preheat the oven to 180°C/350°F/Gas 4. If you're cooking outdoors, make a fire, let it burn down and then place your Dutch oven or casserole dish on the resulting embers (see page 10). Use the hob (stove) if cooking indoors.

To make the filling, heat the olive oil in the Dutch oven over your chosen heat source. Add the onion and garlic and allow them to sauté for a couple of minutes before adding the leek. Continue to sauté for about 10 minutes, stirring occasionally. Stir in the thyme and cook for a minute or two more before stirring in the mushrooms and adding a pinch of salt and black pepper. Cook for about 3–4 minutes and then stir in the artichoke hearts. Continue to cook for a further couple of minutes then add the wine or beer, if using. Keep cooking, stirring occasionally, for another 5 minutes and if it starts to catch, just add a splash of water. Season again to taste, then stir in the cream and cook for a final couple of minutes before stirring in the parsley. Remove from the heat and place to one side.

Roll the pastry out on a floured surface until it's about 3mm/⅛in thick, then use the lid of your Dutch oven or casserole dish to cut out a circle. Place the pastry circle directly on top of the pie filling and prick it in a few places with a fork. Brush with about half of the whisked egg and then either place in the oven for about 35 minutes, uncovered, or, if you're outdoors, cover with a lid and put the Dutch oven into the embers. Cover the lid with hot charcoal or wood embers (see page 12) and leave to bake until the pastry is cooked. As always, this is not an exact science but will probably take 30–40 minutes. Bake until the pastry lid is golden brown. Be careful when lifting the lid to check on progress. Dave uses an old metal tent peg and an oven glove.

SMOKY COWBOY BEANS WITH CAMPFIRE DAMPERS

SERVES 4

Another campfire classic, a big pot of these cowboy beans, aka *frijoles charros*, is a lovely way to end a day outdoors. Dampers make it more of a communal dipping affair and are a very easy campfire bread. They're also nice with a little grated cheese, or you can, in other moments, substitute the salt and oregano for sugar and use to dip into jams and spreads. They're very popular with children! This dish is also good served with brown rice and guacamole, and sour cream is always a delicious option.

For the smoky cowboy beans

1 red pepper

2 tbsp coconut oil

1 large white onion, chopped

2 garlic cloves, thinly sliced

1 dried chipotle chilli, soaked in hot water for 15 minutes, drained and chopped

½ tsp ground cumin

½ tsp smoked paprika

pinch of salt

2 tbsp tomato purée (tomato paste)

1 x 400-g/14-oz can chopped tomatoes

2 x 400-g/14-oz cans pinto beans, drained and rinsed

handful coriander (cilantro), chopped

2 limes, halved, to serve

For the dampers

250g/9oz/2 cups wholemeal self-raising (self-rising) flour

½ tbsp dried oregano

pinch of salt

175ml/5¾fl oz/¾ cup water

8 skewers or sticks

Poke a few holes in the red pepper and place it directly on the barbecue grill, or on the open flame of the hob, turning every minute or so until it's completely blackened. Place the blackened pepper in a container with a tight lid and leave to sweat for 10 minutes. By this time you should be able to easily remove the black skin. Cut the peeled pepper in half, remove the seeds, slice and set aside.

Heat the coconut oil in a Dutch oven or large pan over your chosen heat source and, when hot, add the onions and cook until translucent before adding the garlic, chilli, cumin, smoked paprika and salt. Continue to cook for a further couple of minutes, stirring continuously, before adding the tomato purée. Cook for another couple of minutes and then stir in the chopped tomatoes, red pepper and pinto beans. Bring to the boil then turn the heat down and simmer for about 30 minutes.

Meanwhile make the dampers by mixing the flour, oregano and salt in a bowl. Gradually stir in the water a little at a time, and then knead until you have a soft dough. Divide into 8 equal pieces, then roll each piece into a thin sausage shape. Wrap your skewers or sticks with a layer of foil (leaving a little space at the end to hold) and then wrap a piece of dough around each skewer in a spiral. When you're ready to eat, place the dough skewers on the grill, or hold over an open flame, turning regularly, until charred and hard to the touch.

Serve the beans with chopped coriander and lime wedges, and the hot dampers on the side.

RAMEN POT

SERVES 2
V

1 litre/35fl oz/4¼ cups water

4g/⅛oz fresh ginger, finely chopped

2 tsp vegetable bouillon powder

3 tsp tamari

20g/¾oz/1 tbsp brown rice miso paste

50g/1¾oz smoked tofu, sliced

60g/2oz frozen edamame
beans, defrosted

50g/1¾oz carrots, julienned

4 thin slices red chilli (or more to taste)

3g/¹⁄₁₆oz dried wakame

8g/¼oz coriander (cilantro), roughly picked

10g/⅓oz dried shiitake mushrooms,
soaked in hot water for 15 minutes,
strained and sliced

½ spring onion (scallion), top and tailed
and sliced on the diagonal

70g/2½oz long-stem broccoli,
finely sliced

90g/3¼oz ramen noodles

These are a great way to have good, nutritious food on the go. You can fill the jars up with most of the ingredients in advance and then just make up a quick stock to finish it off when you're ready to eat. They work really well for camping or activities like bicycle touring. You'll need a couple of jars with lids; we just use Kilner or old gherkin jars that hold about 650ml/22fl oz/2¾ cups.

First make a stock. Bring the water to the boil in a Dutch oven or large pan. Add the ginger, bouillon powder and tamari and bring back to the boil. Remove from the heat and stir in the miso paste.

In each jar, place half of the smoked tofu slices, edamame, carrots, chilli slices, wakame, coriander, mushrooms and spring onion.

Add the broccoli and noodles to the stock and return to the heat until the stock is just short of boiling. Divide the broccoli and noodles between each jar and pour enough of the stock into each jar to cover all the ingredients. Seal with a lid and leave for about 3–5 minutes to heat through before eating.

TRUFFLED MAC & CHEESE WITH PORCINI MUSHROOMS

SERVES 4

A classic member of a barbecue spread, the truffle oil and porcini mushroom sprinkle make this mac and cheese just a little bit more special. The panko (Japanese-style) breadcrumbs make sure it's got plenty of those lovely crispy bits.

If cooking indoors, preheat the oven to 180°C/350°F/Gas 4.

Place your Dutch oven or casserole dish over your chosen outdoor heat source, or the hob (stove) if cooking indoors, and heat the milk until it's nearly boiling. Transfer to a bowl and place to one side. Melt the butter in the Dutch oven before stirring in the flour with a wooden spoon to make a roux. It's ready for the next step when it starts to look a little brown (after about 3–5 minutes). At that point, remove the pan from the heat and whisk in the hot milk a little at a time.

Return to the heat and carry on whisking continuously until the mixture thickens up. Remove from the heat again and stir in the mustard, then the cheese and a little salt and white pepper to taste. Stir until the cheese has melted, returning the pan briefly to the heat if needed. Add the macaroni and mix thoroughly so all the macaroni is well coated with the cheese sauce. Sprinkle over the panko and, if you're cooking indoors, transfer to the oven without a lid and bake for about 30 minutes until golden brown. If you're cooking outdoors, put a lid on top of the Dutch oven and place it over the embers, covering the lid with hot charcoals or embers (see page 12). Bake until golden brown.

Towards the end of the cooking time, place a skillet on your heat source and heat the olive oil before adding the shallots and garlic. Sauté until they take on a nice brown colour and then add the mushrooms. Continue to sauté for a further couple of minutes, stirring occasionally. Add a little salt and white pepper, stir in the truffle oil and parsley and remove immediately from the heat.

When the mac and cheese is ready, top with the mushroom mixture and serve.

1.2 litres/40fl oz/5 cups whole milk

50g/1¾oz/3½ tbsp butter

50g/1¾oz/6 tbsp plain (all-purpose) flour

1 tsp Dijon mustard

200g/7oz mature Cheddar (sharp) cheese, grated

salt and white pepper

400g/14oz macaroni, cooked until al dente

20g/¾oz/½ cup panko breadcrumbs

2 tbsp olive oil

40g/1½oz shallots, thinly sliced

1 garlic clove, roughly chopped

40g/1½oz dried porcini mushrooms, soaked in hot water for 15 minutes, strained and roughly chopped

2 tsp white truffle oil

10g/⅓oz parsley, roughly chopped

BUNNY CHOW

SERVES 4–6
VO

Having grown up in Durban, Dave has strong childhood memories of this dish. It originated among the Indian South Africans who needed a cheap and practical way to take their lunch curry to the fields. So traditionally the curry part of a 'bunny' is served in a hollowed-out loaf of white bread that, as well as being strong, also stands in for a roti. It's pretty delicious served that way but we have chosen to use individual rolls for this recipe. It's up to you.

3 tbsp vegetable oil
1 onion, chopped
3 garlic cloves, crushed
30g/1oz fresh ginger, peeled and chopped
1 tsp ground coriander
2 tsp garam masala
1 tsp ground turmeric
½ tsp ground cumin
½ handful curry leaves
1 long red chilli, finely chopped
3 plum tomatoes, chopped
450g/1lb cauliflower, cut into florets
750ml/26fl oz/3¼ cups vegetable stock
2 x 400-g/14-oz cans chickpeas, drained and rinsed
200g/7oz kale, picked
salt and black pepper

To serve
6 bread rolls, crusty are best (omit if wheat- and gluten-free, or use free-from)
mango chutney
crème fraîche
6 sprigs coriander (cilantro), picked

If cooking outdoors, prepare a heat source for your Dutch oven or pot and begin to heat. If indoors, place a Dutch oven on the hob (stove) over a medium-high heat.

Heat the vegetable oil, then add the onion, garlic and ginger and sauté for about 5 minutes until the onions start to appear translucent. Stir in the ground coriander, garam masala, turmeric, cumin, curry leaves and red chilli and continue to cook for another couple of minutes before adding the tomatoes and continuing for a further couple of minutes. Add the cauliflower florets and cook for a minute or so before pouring in the vegetable stock. Stir well and then add the chickpeas; stir again and leave to cook for about 25–35 minutes, checking occasionally, until most of the liquid has been absorbed.

When the chickpea curry is ready, stir in the kale and continue to cook for a further 5–10 minutes. Season to taste with salt and black pepper.

Hollow out the rolls (but keep the insides for dunking), then stuff with the curry and add a little mango chutney, crème fraîche and coriander on the top.

Vegan option Omit the crème fraîche or use a plant-based alternative.

JOLLOF POT

SERVES 4–6
V / WF / GF

4 tbsp olive oil
1 onion, sliced
3 garlic cloves, crushed
30g/1oz fresh ginger, peeled and chopped
1 long red chilli, finely sliced
2 tsp hot smoked paprika
500g/1lb 2oz/3¼ cups brown basmati rice
1 litre/35fl oz/4¼ cups vegetable stock
4 plum tomatoes, chopped
1 x 400-g/14-oz can tomatoes
10 okra, cut in half lengthways
20g/¾oz coriander (cilantro), chopped
salt and black pepper

This West African spicy one-pot rice is traditionally a side dish but we find it satisfying on it's own; although it's also great at a barbecue served with something like the seitan jerky (see page 70) or yakitori skewers (see page 71). This recipe is already pretty fiery, but substitute the long red chilli for the more traditionally used Scotch bonnet if you're feeling hardcore.

If cooking outdoors, prepare a heat source for your Dutch oven or pot and begin to heat. If indoors, place a Dutch oven on the hob (stove) over a medium-high heat.

Heat the olive oil, then add the onion, garlic and ginger and sauté for about 5 minutes until the onions start to appear translucent. Stir in the chilli and paprika and continue to cook for 1–2 minutes. Stir in the rice and continue to cook for another minute or two before adding in the stock and the plum and canned tomatoes. Stir well, then cover with a lid and cook for about 15 minutes. Add the okra, replace the lid and continue to cook for a further 15–20 minutes until the rice is cooked, checking occasionally. Add a little more water if at any point the mixture starts to look too dry but the rice is not yet cooked.

When it's ready, remove from the heat, stir through the coriander and season to taste with salt and black pepper.

HAY-SMOKED GOAT'S CHEESE

MAKES
1 CHEESE
WF / GF

This one doesn't need a fire, but you do need a pot with a secure lid that can handle fire – cast iron is best, if possible – and ideally a blowtorch. We love the taste of the hay smoke (which we just pick up from our local pet shop), but you can also experiment with this technique by using pine needles, thyme, lavender, smoked woods, the list goes on... The cheese looks great served on a piece of wood, and you can either use it in recipes where you want to add a nice bonfire flavour or simply enjoy it on it's own with crackers and grapes. You can use any cheese or anything else you'd like to smoke!

3 handfuls hay
1 goat's cheese (approx 125g/4½oz)

Place the hay in your pot or Dutch oven. Lay the cheese on top of the hay, in the middle. Set the hay on fire, ideally using a blowtorch, but if you don't have one, just persevere with matches.

When the hay is ignited and there's lots of smoke, quickly put the lid on and, depending on how tightly the lid fits, you could also seal with clingfilm to contain all the smoke. Leave for 10–15 minutes, then remove the cheese.

RICE 'N' PEAS

A Caribbean classic, the 'peas' referred to are actually kidney beans, although you can certainly enjoy experimenting with other types. We particularly like black beans as an alternative.

This is a great dish to have up your sleeve as it goes with pretty much everything, and at a veggie barbecue we tend to serve it alongside things like skewers or salads.

Scotch bonnets are always used traditionally, but here we've made it optional, as while they do certainly add flavour they're also super spicy.

SERVES 4
AS A SIDE
V / WF / GF

3 tbsp coconut oil

1½ onions, chopped

2 garlic cloves, finely chopped

500g/1lb 2oz/2¾ cups long-grain brown rice

1 tsp dried thyme

1.5 litres/52fl oz/6½ cups vegetable stock

1 Scotch bonnet chilli (optional)

1 x 400-g/14-oz can kidney beans, drained and rinsed

salt and black pepper

In your Dutch oven or pot, either over the fire or on the hob (stove), heat the coconut oil before adding the onions. Sauté for a couple of minutes until translucent, then add the garlic, rice and thyme and continue to sauté for another couple of minutes, stirring constantly.

Add the vegetable stock and whole Scotch bonnet, if using, cover the pot with a lid and bring to the boil. Allow it to boil for 25–30 minutes, or until you can no longer see any stock. At this point, carefully locate and remove the chilli, if you've used it, and then mix in the beans.

Turn down the heat to a simmer if you're indoors, but otherwise just continue to heat until the rice is fully cooked. This should take around 10–15 minutes. Season to taste with salt and black pepper.

STREUSEL-TOPPED STEWED APPLE & QUINCE

SERVES 4
VO

The streusel topping is made in advance and brought to the barbecue, which makes it easy to quickly rustle up a hearty crumble-style dessert outdoors. Quince is a lovely fruit to use and adds an unusual tart yet floral dimension.

For the streusel topping
100g/3½oz/¾ cup plain (all-purpose) flour
100g/3½oz/½ cup unrefined brown sugar
1 tsp ground cinnamon
20g/¾oz/2 tbsp pumpkin seeds
pinch of salt
35g/1¼oz/2½ tbsp butter, slightly softened

For the stewed fruits
200ml/7fl oz/scant 1 cup water
1 quince, peeled, quartered and cored
75g/2¾oz/6 tbsp unrefined brown sugar
½ tsp vanilla extract
1 tsp ground cinnamon
2 Bramley apples or cooking apple of choice, cored, cut into large chunks and placed in a bowl of water (so they don't go brown)

cream or ice cream, to serve (optional)

If cooking indoors, preheat the oven to 180°C/350°F/Gas 4.

To make the streusel topping, place the flour, sugar, cinnamon, pumpkin seeds, salt and butter in a mixing bowl and use your fingertips to mix it all together until it resembles crumbs. Line a baking sheet with greaseproof (waxed) paper and then tip the mixture into it and gently spread. Bake for about 30 minutes until it's taken on some colour and is crunchy. Leave to cool and then transfer to a sealed jar until needed.

To make the stewed fruits, place the water into a Dutch oven or pan and place on your chosen outdoor heat source, or on the hob (stove) over a medium heat if cooking indoors. Add the quince, sugar, vanilla and cinnamon and cook for about 10–12 minutes until the quince starts to soften, stirring occasionally. Drain the apples, add them to the pan and continue cooking for a further 5–8 minutes until everything is soft. Give it a good final mix, then transfer to bowls and top with the streusel and your choice of cream or ice cream.

Vegan option Substitute the butter for a plant-based spread and choose vegan cream or ice cream.

SKILLET

PULLED JACKFRUIT BURGERS WITH BARBECUED PINEAPPLE

SERVES 4
V / WF / GF
(WITHOUT
THE BUN)

Jackfruit is one of those strange-looking Asian fruits that can be hard to know quite what to do with, but these days it's common in canned form, which is a very easy way to use it. This pulled jackfruit mix is also great in tacos or burritos.

Begin by making the pulled jackfruit. Gently heat the olive oil in a skillet or pan and sauté the onions for a couple of minutes. Add the garlic and the jackfruit and continue to sauté gently for about 10 minutes until they all just start to brown.

Add all the other jackfruit ingredients except for the barbecue sauce, then stir well and cover. Bring to the boil, then turn down the heat and simmer for about 35–40 minutes or until all the liquid has been absorbed. Check it every 10 minutes or so to ensure it isn't sticking, and if there is any liquid left after 40 minutes, simply remove the lid and keep cooking until the liquid has gone.

Using a potato masher, lightly mash the jackfruit to the point that it begins to break apart and starts to resemble pulled meat. Place to one side.

Meanwhile, make the barbecued pineapple. Rub a little olive oil on both sides of each slice with your finger. Place the slices on the grill if outdoors, or in a very hot griddle plate if indoors, and grill until you have good colour on both sides. Place to one side.

When you're ready to serve, put the pulled jackfruit back over a gentle heat. Once it's begun to take on some heat and colour, spoon over 4–5 tablespoons of the barbecue sauce. Mix well and continue to cook until thoroughly heated.

Load the buns with some lettuce leaves, a generous amount of the pulled jackfruit, an extra dollop of the barbecue sauce, if you like, a slice or two of the barbecued pineapple and a spoonful of the rainbow slaw.

For the pulled jackfruit

4 tbsp olive oil

2 small onions, chopped

4 garlic cloves, crushed

2 x 400-g/14-oz cans jackfruit in water, drained and cut into quarters

500ml/17fl oz/generous 2 cups vegetable stock

2 tsp chopped thyme

½ chipotle chilli, soaked in hot water for 15 minutes, drained and chopped

2 tbsp apple cider vinegar

2 tsp tamari

2 tbsp blackstrap molasses

½ tsp mustard powder

pinch of black pepper

1 batch chipotle barbecue sauce (see page 113)

For the barbecued pineapple

1 pineapple, peeled, cored and cut into slices about 2cm/¾in thick

1 tbsp olive oil

To serve

4 burger buns of choice, halved and toasted

1 head little gem lettuce

1 batch rainbow slaw (see page 101)

For the refried beans

1 tbsp olive oil

1 small onion, chopped

1 garlic clove, crushed

pinch of ground cinnamon

½ tsp ground cumin

salt and black pepper

1 x 400-g/14-oz can black beans, drained and rinsed

zest of ½ lime

juice of ¼ lime

For the tomato sauce

1 tbsp olive oil

1 small onion, chopped

1 garlic clove, crushed

1 red pepper, deseeded and sliced lengthways

300g/10½oz cherry or plum tomatoes, roughly chopped

1 dried ancho chilli (should weigh about 15g/½oz)

1 bay leaf

For the rest

4 eggs

75g/2¾oz feta cheese, crumbled

1 avocado, peeled, pitted and roughly sliced

zest of ½ lime

juice of ¼ lime

a few sprigs coriander (cilantro), leaves picked

4–6 pure corn tortillas

1 lime, cut into wedges, to serve

ONE-SKILLET HUEVOS RANCHEROS

SERVES 2–4
WF / GF

Translated as 'rancher's eggs', this is a mighty campfire breakfast to power you through any hard day's slog. But really it's great at any time of the day and we love anything that can be done in one dish. It's traditionally served with fried eggs, but when we're in the outdoors we prefer to poach the eggs in the skillet (as below) for ease.

Begin by making the refried beans. Heat a skillet on your chosen outdoor heat source, or on the hob (stove) if cooking indoors. Add the olive oil followed by the onion and sauté for a couple of minutes until translucent. Add the garlic, cinnamon, cumin and a little salt and pepper and sauté for another couple of minutes. Add the black beans and continue to cook for about 10 minutes, crushing them as they cook with a potato masher. If it gets too dry at any stage, just add a splash of water. Finish by mixing in the lime zest and juice and transfer to a bowl until needed.

Reheat the skillet and add the olive oil for the tomato sauce before adding the onion and garlic. Sauté

for about 3–4 minutes until they begin to caramelize, then add the sliced red pepper and continue to sauté for another 5 minutes, or until it all starts to take on some nice colour. Add the tomatoes, the whole ancho chilli, the bay leaf and a pinch of salt and pepper along with about 100ml/3½fl oz/scant ½ cup water. Cover and cook for about 10 minutes, stirring occasionally. Remove the chilli and the bay leaf and then take the skillet off the heat.

Chop half of the removed chilli and stir it back into the skillet (you can add more if you're a chilli fiend but this is a comfortable amount). Now make four little indents in the tomato sauce and crack an egg into each.

Return to the heat, cover once again and cook for about 3–5 minutes until the eggs are cooked to your liking. Take off the heat once more.

Remove the lid, sprinkle over the feta, then add the avocado, lime zest and juice, and the coriander.

Quickly heat the tortillas by popping them on the grill for a minute or two until you have some char lines.

To serve, use each tortilla as a base and pile up with the refried beans and a generous amount of the skillet contents. You can't go wrong with an additional wedge of lime to serve.

SKILLET ASPARAGUS WITH LEMON & MUSTARD

SERVES 2
VO / WF / GF

100ml/3½fl oz/scant ½ cup water
250g/9oz asparagus, woody ends removed
2 tbsp olive oil
30g/1oz/2 tbsp wholegrain mustard
30ml/1fl oz/2 tbsp lemon juice
1 tsp honey
salt and black pepper

Asparagus season is definitely one of our favourite times of year, and it's definitely one of our favourite things to quickly prepare on a skillet as a knockout side dish or snack.

Heat the skillet on your chosen outdoor heat source, or on the hob (stove) if indoors, then add the water and the asparagus and cook with a lid on for about 5 minutes until the asparagus is just tender. Strain off any excess water and then add the olive oil, mustard, lemon juice, honey and a generous pinch of salt and pepper.

Continue to cook, stirring occasionally for another couple of minutes until it's all well combined and the asparagus is cooked to your preference. Pour into a side dish to serve.

Vegan option Omit the honey.

NORTHERN-STYLE CORNBREAD

SERVES 4
AS A SIDE

115g/4oz/½ cup butter
125g/4½oz/scant 1 cup plain white
(all-purpose) flour
125g/4½oz/¾ cup cornmeal
40g/1½oz/3¼ tbsp unrefined brown sugar
1 tsp baking powder
½ tsp bicarbonate of soda (baking soda)
pinch of salt
240ml/9fl oz/1 cup buttermilk
50g/1¾oz/about 3 tbsp honey
2 eggs

A classic American dish, there is fierce debate about whether or not to include a sweetener, with the South saying nay and the North saying yea. We've both got a sweet tooth (and love a sweet and savoury combo) so are in the northern camp, but just omit the honey if you prefer. Great at the campfire as an accompaniment to chillies and stews, but also pretty darn yummy on it's own with a bit of butter.

Preheat the oven to 200°C/400°F/Gas 6 or, if outdoors, prepare a heat source for your skillet and make sure you'll have some embers for later.

Place the skillet on your chosen heat source to melt the butter and then pour most of the butter into a small bowl, leaving just a trace in the skillet.

In another bowl, whisk together the flour, cornmeal, sugar, baking powder, bicarbonate of soda and salt.

And in another bowl whisk together the buttermilk, honey and eggs.

Pour the egg mixture and the butter into the dry mixture and whisk thoroughly until well combined but not over-mixed.

Gently heat the skillet, then remove from the heat and add all of the bread mixture. Smooth it out so it's evenly distributed and then place in the oven for about 20 minutes. If you're outdoors, cover with a lid and bake Dutch-oven style (see page 12). In either case, the bread is ready when it's risen and fluffy like a sponge cake but a bit crisp on the outside. And it's definitely best served hot!

For the sour cherries
150ml/5fl oz/scant ⅔ cup water
150g/5½oz/¾ cup unrefined brown sugar
½ tsp vanilla extract
1 cinnamon stick
300g/10½oz frozen sour cherries

For the sweet crème fraîche
200g/7oz/scant 1 cup crème fraîche
8g/¼oz/1 tbsp icing (confectioners') sugar

For the hotcakes
100g/3½oz/¾ cup wholemeal self-raising
(self-rising) flour
25g/1oz/2 tbsp unrefined brown sugar
100ml/3½fl oz/scant ½ cup milk
1 egg
10g/⅓oz/2 tsp butter

CAMPFIRE HOTCAKES WITH SOUR CHERRIES & SWEET CRÈME FRAÎCHE

MAKES
ABOUT 8–10
SMALL
HOTCAKES

Fresh cherries are always wonderful but we've never managed to stop the birds from eating all the cherries on our tree, so we tend to use frozen sour cherries for convenience, or also if it's the wrong time of year. This is an excellent camping breakfast but you can make the cherries and crème fraîche ahead of time to bring with you if that's easier. If you do use fresh or can't get sour cherries, you might want to slightly reduce the sugar to taste.

When cooking the hotcakes, especially if outdoors, you don't want the skillet to get too hot, so just move it to the side of the grill if you need it to cool down.

Begin by making the sour cherry mix. Place the water, brown sugar, vanilla and cinnamon stick in a pan and gently bring to the boil. Add the cherries and bring back up to the boil, stirring occasionally. Taste the cherries to make sure they're cooked through and when they are, remove from the heat and place to one side until needed.

Put the crème fraîche and icing sugar together in a bowl and mix well to combine. Again, place to one side until needed.

Make the hotcakes by mixing the flour and sugar in a bowl. Then, in another bowl, lightly whisk the milk and egg. Pour that into the first bowl and give it all a good mix until you have a fairly thick pancake batter.

Heat a skillet on your chosen outdoor heat source (or on the hob/stove on a fairly low heat if cooking indoors) Add the butter and allow it to melt, then pour the melted butter into the hotcake batter and mix. Use a piece of paper towel to coat the skillet with what butter remains and return to the heat.

Drop about 1 tablespoon of the batter per hotcake into the skillet and leave to cook until you start to see bubbles on the surface of the batter. Use a palette knife to turn the cakes over and continue to cook for about 2–3 minutes until golden brown on the other side too. You may need to do this in batches.

Serve the cakes piping hot in a stack along with the cherries and a generous dollop of the sweet crème fraîche.

BROWN SUGAR BURNT FIGS WITH MASCARPONE & FLAKED ALMONDS

SERVES 2
WF / GF

This is such an easy one-skillet dessert, ideal for making over a fire and enjoying outdoors. The previous keeper of our allotment was Greek and so we inherited an abundance of fig trees, which always leaves us with a glut in the summer. This is a perfect way for us to enjoy them in situ and just moments after they've been picked. If you don't have figs, you can alternatively use many other kinds of fruits; pitted nectarines, peaches or plums are all great cooked in this way too.

There's a fine line when it comes to burning (it goes against every rule of Dave's chef training), but you do need to hold your nerve and not move the figs around for long enough to achieve that depth of flavour only something a little blackened can achieve.

20g/¾oz/¼ cup flaked (sliced) almonds
30g/1oz/2½ tbsp unrefined brown sugar
6 fresh figs, halved
zest of ½ lemon, plus extra to garnish
½ sprig rosemary, woody part removed, plus a couple of sprigs to garnish
1 tsp vanilla extract
20g/¾oz/1½ tbsp butter
100g/3½oz/scant ½ cup mascarpone, to serve

Heat a skillet on your chosen outdoor heat source, or on the hob (stove) if cooking indoors. Add the flaked almonds and toast for a minute or so, continuously moving them around, then transfer them to a bowl and place to one side. Temporarily remove the skillet from the heat.

Put the sugar in a bowl and dip the cut side of each fig half into the sugar so they're well coated. Leave them in the bowl with any remaining sugar and mix in the lemon zest, rosemary and vanilla. Place the skillet back on the heat, melt the butter, then arrange the figs, cut side down, around the skillet and spoon over anything remaining in the bowl. Let the figs begin to burn, which should take about 5 minutes, before flipping them over to do the same on the other side for a couple of minutes. Flip them over once again and cook until things have got a bit smoky and really well caramelized. If at any point the mixture starts to get too thick or caramelizes too soon, just add a splash of water and continue.

Remove the skillet from the heat and transfer the figs to a serving dish. Add a dash of water to the remains of the skillet and then drizzle that liquid over the figs.

Top with the toasted flaked almonds, a little more lemon zest, a generous spoonful of mascarpone and a sprig of rosemary.

CARAMELIZED BANANAS WITH VANILLA ICE CREAM

SERVES 2–4
WF / GF

Another super-easy one-skillet dessert, this recipe is great proof that sometimes you really can't beat simplicity. We were first served a version of it by our good friend Ananda, the chef and manager at the amazing Last House in Sri Lanka, and we've been regularly making it at home ever since. If you want your friends to go 'yum', this is the one!

60ml/2fl oz/¼ cup water
60g/2oz/5 tbsp unrefined brown sugar
4 bananas, peeled and cut into about 3-cm/1¼-in pieces
½ tsp vanilla extract
20g/¾oz/1½ tbsp butter
vanilla ice cream, to serve

Heat a skillet on your chosen outdoor heat source (or on the hob/stove if cooking indoors), then add the water and sugar and heat, stirring occasionally, until the sugar has dissolved. Add the bananas and vanilla extract and gently stir. Cook for about 5–10 minutes, moving the bananas around, until they appear soft, adding little splashes of water as needed if the caramel starts to look too thick or as if it's going to burn.

Add the butter and when it's melted and mixed through, spoon the bananas into bowls and add a generous amount of vanilla ice cream. Serve immediately.

As a final touch, you can add a little water to the used skillet and heat until the water has reduced down, then drizzle the sticky remains over the bananas and ice cream.

LEMONGRASS SKILLET BRÛLÉE

500ml/17fl oz/generous 2 cups double (heavy) cream

3 lemongrass sticks, pounded, cut into pieces and then finely shredded

½ tsp vanilla extract

6 egg yolks

55g/2oz/4½ tbsp light brown sugar, plus 40g/1½oz/3¼ tbsp for topping

butter, for greasing

punnet (tray) of raspberries or redcurrants, to serve (optional)

This is probably one to cook at home, but you can take the chilled custard in your skillet to the barbecue and finish it there by either burning the sugar topping with a blow torch or getting another skillet red hot and bringing it down onto the sugar. This is delicious served with some fresh raspberries or redcurrants. We use a 20-cm/8-in skillet for this one.

Preheat the oven to 160°C/315°F/Gas 2–3.

Place the cream, lemongrass and vanilla extract in a pan and heat gently until it just reaches a simmer. Remove from the heat and leave to one side. Meanwhile, place the egg yolks and the 55g/2oz sugar in a bowl and whisk thoroughly. Strain the warmed cream into the egg mixture and give it all a good whisk.

Very lightly grease your skillet (or ovenproof frying pan) with the butter and pour in the egg and cream mixture. Place the skillet in a deep roasting pan and make a bain-marie by adding water to the roasting pan until it comes halfway up the skillet. Place carefully in the oven and bake for 20–25 minutes until the custard is just set but still has a bit of a wobble in the middle.

Carefully transfer the skillet to a shallow icy bath so the brûlée doesn't continue to cook in the pan. Once cool, transfer to the fridge until fully chilled.

Spread the remaining 40g/1½oz sugar over the cold custard and burn with a blow torch (or you could alternatively make the base of another skillet very hot and bring it down for about 15 seconds on top of the sugar). Serve with some raspberries or redcurrants, if using.

GRILL

SABICH SANDWICH

SERVES 4

This was a revelation on a recent trip to Tel Aviv. In fact, the entire trip to Tel Aviv was a foodie revelation but this was definitely a highlight. It was originally brought to Israel in the 1940s by Iraqi Jews who used to eat its key elements on Shabbat, when no cooking is allowed; they could still produce a sustaining meal by using precooked aubergine (traditionally fried, but here we're using our grill), boiled potatoes and eggs. In Israel, somebody clever put it all into a pita bread with a few other flavoursome additions and so a most excellent street food was born, and kiosks began to appear around the city. The main ingredients of a sabich are also sometimes served in salad form and that's another great option if you want to leave out the bread or create a big sharing bowl.

300g/10½oz aubergine (eggplant), cut lengthways into 5-mm/¼-in thick slices
salt and black pepper
300g/10½oz white cabbage, shredded
2 tbsp white wine vinegar
olive oil, to drizzle
4–8 wholewheat pita breads

To serve
mango chutney
1 batch tahini sauce (see page 123)
8 new potatoes, boiled and sliced
1 batch Israeli salad (see page 92)
120g/4½oz pickles of your choice (shop-bought or see pages 115 or 118),
4 eggs, boiled and sliced
zhoug (see page 124) or other spicy sauce

Place the aubergine slices on a cold grill or wire rack set over a roasting pan or tray. Sprinkle both sides with a little salt to draw out the water and leave for about 15 minutes.

Meanwhile, place the shredded cabbage in a bowl and add a little salt and black pepper and the white wine vinegar. Leave to one side.

When they're ready, wipe the aubergine slices with paper towels to remove the water and excess salt, then drizzle with a little olive oil. Place the aubergine slices on a hot grill for 3–5 minutes on each side until you have some good char lines. Remove from the heat and leave to one side.

Place the pitas on the hot grill, turning occasionally, until they're warm on both sides. Cut lengthways to create a pocket ready for stuffing.

To serve, stuff each pita to taste, starting with a thin layer of mango chutney, then adding the tahini sauce, shredded cabbage, sliced potatoes, Israeli salad, pickles, grilled aubergine, sliced egg, a little more tahini sauce and a drizzle of zhoug or other hot sauce to finish. Or, alternatively, we tend to prefer to put all the elements out and leave people to create their own.

BARBECUED VEGETABLES WITH CHIMICHURRI

SERVES 4
V / WF / GF

1 bunch asparagus, woody ends removed

1 aubergine (eggplant), cut lengthways into 5-mm/¼-in slices

2 courgettes (zucchini), cut lengthways into 5-mm/¼-in slices

2 red peppers (we like to use Romano peppers), halved

1 bunch spring onions (scallions), topped and tailed

1 fennel bulb, halved, and woody part of stalk removed

2 plum tomatoes, halved

5 tbsp olive oil

salt and black pepper

1 batch chimichurri (see page 110)

This is a simple way to really enjoy the flavours of summer's best vegetables. We've used here some of our favourites, but it works with any vegetable you fancy or happen to have to hand. It's great served as part of a larger barbecue spread with some brown rice and a few easy sides.

Place all the vegetables in a large bowl or on a tray, pour over the olive oil and sprinkle with a generous amount of salt and pepper. Mix gently with your hands to distribute the oil and seasoning.

Once the grill is hot (or use a griddle plate if cooking indoors), work in batches to grill the vegetables until they're nicely charred on both sides. The different vegetables will take slightly different times to char, so do keep an eye on them and remove them from the grill when they are done.

Arrange on a serving platter, pour over the chimichurri and enjoy!

ELOTES (MEXICAN STREET CORN WITH GARLIC MAYONNAISE & CRUMBLED FETA)

SERVES 4
GF / WF

60g/2oz/¼ cup sour cream
60g/2oz/¼ cup mayonnaise
120g/4½oz feta cheese, crumbled
1 garlic clove, crushed
¼ tsp red chilli flakes, plus a little extra to garnish (optional)
1 tbsp chopped coriander (cilantro), plus a little extra to garnish
4 ears of corn, shucked
1 lime, quartered, to serve

A highlight of any trip to Mexico, this is our absolute favourite way to enjoy corn on the cob and is a star player in any barbecue spread or a winning standalone snack. It is undeniably messy to eat, but that's definitely part of its joy! You can use ready-prepared corn on the cob if it's too much of a faff to shuck your own, but the ears on fresh corn do look good, and they are also very useful for holding.

In a mixing bowl, combine the sour cream, mayonnaise and crumbled feta. Stir in the crushed garlic, chilli flakes and coriander and place to one side.

Place the corn on your grill (or under the grill if you're using an oven) and rotate every now and again until all sides have a lovely char and you begin to hear the occasional kernel popping.

Remove from the grill and slather generously with the cheese mixture. Garnish with a little extra chopped coriander, a few more chilli flakes, if desired, and a wedge of lime.

STICKY TEMPEH 'RIBS'

SERVES 2–4
V

Ubiquitous throughout Indonesia, we're always surprised not to see more tempeh in the UK, but you can generally find it in health food shops, sometimes in the freezer section. These 'ribs' are a great part of a veggie barbecue and work well served with rice and Asian greens, or our rainbow slaw (see page 101). Kecap manis, an Indonesian sweet soy sauce, is one of our star condiments and is available in most Asian grocers. It's thick like treacle and absolutely delicious added to stir-fries and rice dishes.

250g/9oz tempeh, cut into 5-mm/¼-in thick slices

For the marinade
1 tsp cumin seeds, toasted
1 tsp coriander seeds, toasted
1 garlic clove, chopped
1½ tbsp olive oil
3 tbsp kecap manis, plus 2 tbsp to serve
1 handful coriander (cilantro), chopped, plus a little extra to garnish

For the salsa
2 small shallots, finely sliced
1 red chilli, deseeded and finely sliced
½ handful coriander (cilantro), chopped
juice and zest of ½ lime
salt and black pepper
2 tbsp kecap manis marinade (see above)

First make the marinade. Place the toasted cumin and coriander seeds in a pestle and mortar and grind until powdered. Add the garlic, grind a little more, then add the olive oil and kecap manis and grind again. Mix in the chopped coriander to finish.

Put the tempeh slices into a large bowl and then pour over the marinade, making sure they're fully coated. Leave to one side for about 15 minutes. Meanwhile, preheat your barbecue or oven grill (broiler).

Put the tempeh slices on/under the grill (place the slices in a roasting pan if cooking indoors) and cook, basting regularly with the leftover marinade and turning as needed to get a nice colour on both sides.

Combine all the salsa ingredients with a little salt and pepper in a bowl.

When the tempeh is ready, serve on a plate and top with the salsa. Drizzle over the additional kecap manis and enjoy!

8–10 metal or bamboo skewers

500g/1lb 2oz aubergine (eggplant), cut into roughly 3-cm/1¼-in cubes

salt and black pepper

1 green pepper, cut into roughly 3-cm/1¼-in squares

2 blocks smoked tofu (about 200g/7oz), cut into roughly 2-cm/¾-in cubes

6 spring onions (scallions), cut into 4-cm/1½-in batons, plus 1 finely sliced to garnish

150g/5½oz shiitake mushrooms, trimmed and cut to a similar size as the other skewer items

2 tbsp vegetable oil, for brushing

65g/2¼oz fresh ginger, peeled and grated

40g/1½oz/2½ tbsp brown rice miso paste

2 tsp sesame oil

1 tbsp tamari

1 tsp brown rice vinegar

1 tsp unrefined brown sugar

1 tbsp sesame seeds, toasted, to serve

MISO-GLAZED AUBERGINE, SHIITAKE & SMOKED TOFU SKEWERS

These are excellent skewers abounding with Asian flavours. We use miso paste all the time for soups, stocks and marinades and are particularly keen on the brown rice miso from Clearspring. We tend to use Taifun smoked tofu.

If cooking indoors, preheat the oven to 220°C/425°F/Gas 7. If cooking outdoors, prepare the grill. Meanwhile, soak the bamboo skewers (if using) in water as this stops them from burning when they hit the barbecue.

Place the aubergine cubes in a large bowl and sprinkle with a couple of pinches of salt. Leave to one side for about 15 minutes to draw out the water. Rinse with cold water in the bowl, then drain in a colander and pat dry with paper towels.

Assemble the skewers, leaving about 7cm/3in free at one end. We thread on a piece of aubergine, then a piece of pepper, smoked tofu, spring onion, shiitake, and so on until the skewer is full. Brush the skewers with the vegetable oil.

If cooking outdoors, place the skewers onto the hot grill and cook until they're almost done on all sides.

If cooking indoors, put the skewers in a roasting pan and cook for about 15 minutes on one side, and then turn and cook for a further 15 minutes until they appear almost done. At the end of the cooking time, turn your oven grill on full blast.

While the skewers are cooking, make a glaze by mixing together the ginger, miso, sesame oil, tamari, rice vinegar, brown sugar and a little salt and black pepper in a bowl.

Once the skewers are nearly cooked, brush liberally with the glaze. Place under the oven grill, or back on the barbecue, and grill, turning regularly, until they're lovely and charred.

To serve, sprinkle over the finely sliced spring onion and toasted sesame seeds.

TOASTED BRIOCHE S'MORES

SERVES 4
(MAKES
8 BUNS)

8 brioche buns, cut open on one side to form a pocket

80g/2¾oz milk chocolate, broken into pieces

16 veggie marshmallows (normal size, some veggie marshmallows come very small so just use more if needed)

8 metal or bamboo skewers

Having to say 'no' to toasted marshmallows was always one of the most difficult aspects of being vegetarian! But recently there's been a whole slew of veggie marshmallows appearing in the shops and we're making up for lost time! Our particular favourites are Dandies (although this does generally involve mail order), but there are many others available online and in health food shops. This is a classic campfire treat, upgraded a little with the addition of brioche in place of graham crackers or digestive biscuits.

Prepare the grill and get a campfire ready (or you can also use a gas flame on the hob/stove).

Stuff the pocket of each brioche bun with an eighth of the chocolate and put 2 marshmallows on each skewer ready for toasting.

Place the brioches onto the grill (or griddle plate if cooking inside) and cook in batches until they've got good colour on both sides and the chocolate has started to melt. Remove from the heat and place to one side while you quickly toast the marshmallows on the campfire or over a gas flame. When they've also got good colour, carefully transfer them from the skewers into the toasted brioche pockets and enjoy!

SHAWARMA-SPICED CELERIAC

5 cardamom pods
2 cloves
½ tsp fennel seeds
1 tbsp cumin seeds
1 tbsp coriander seeds
pinch of red chilli flakes
½ tsp ground allspice
½ tsp ground cinnamon
½ tsp ground ginger
½ tsp ground turmeric
1½ tsp salt
½ tsp black pepper
1 tbsp unrefined brown sugar
3 tbsp olive oil
800g/1¾lb celeriac (celery root),
peeled and cut into thin slices
(ideally using a mandoline)

To serve
8 pitas, or 1 batch laffa (see page 72)
houmous
pickles of your choice
sauce of your choice (sweet chilli
or zhoug, for example)

Noma mark two now has a fully vegetarian season and one of the standout dishes is a proper looking doner kebab fashioned entirely from celeriac. We've taken inspiration (plus we had a bumper year for celeriac on our allotment) but have gone full-on street food rather than Noma-style. You can always make the shawarma spice mix in advance at home to take with you and it's a rub that works well with lots of other things too.

Prepare the grill if cooking outdoors.

Either in a dry frying pan on the hob (stove) or, if outdoors, using a dry skillet on the grill, lightly toast the cardamom pods, cloves, fennel, and cumin and coriander seeds, then place to one side in a bowl to cool. Grind thoroughly with a pestle and mortar, removing the shells of the cardamom pods, then grind in the red chilli flakes, allspice, cinnamon, ginger, turmeric, salt, black pepper and sugar.

Put the olive oil in a large bowl, then add the celeriac slices and move them around so they're coated in the oil. Gradually add generous amounts of the spice mix and combine by hand until the celeriac slices are well covered (you don't have to use all the spice mix if you want a lighter coating). Leave to infuse for about 10 minutes.

If grilling outdoors, place the celeriac slices on the grill and cook in batches. Turn as needed to get good colour on both sides. If cooking indoors, place the slices on a griddle plate on the gas hob and prepare in the same way as outdoors. When they're ready you can either keep them as they are or roughly chop so they more closely resemble shredded meat.

Lightly grill the pitas or laffa, make a pocket and stuff some of the slices or shreds of celeriac into each one. Load them up with houmous and your choice of pickles and sauces to taste.

SEITAN BBQ 'JERKY'

Seitan is a meat replacement that seems to have become very fashionable in the UK recently but has actually been a staple of Asian cuisine for more than 1,000 years. It's made from just gluten, and now that it's possible to find the key ingredient, vital wheat gluten flour, in most health food shops and online, it couldn't be easier to make your own. The other ingredient you'll need a health food shop (or the internet) for is Engevita yeast flakes, which is a great vegan staple to get to know to add a savoury, almost cheesy flavour to lots of dishes. Here we use our barbecue sauce as the marinade, but you can use whatever barbecue sauce you like. You'll need to make the first part of this at home, but then it's a great dish to take with you to be finished off on the barbecue. Serve with rice dishes and salads.

SERVES
2–4 AS PART
OF A MEAL
V

125g/4½oz/scant 1 cup vital wheat gluten flour
salt and black pepper
½ tsp ground cumin
½ tsp hot smoked paprika
2 tbsp Engevita yeast flakes
1 tsp dried oregano
1 tbsp gram flour
½ tsp onion salt
1 tsp garlic powder
1 tbsp tahini
1 tsp tamari
1 tsp vegetable bouillon powder
150ml/5fl oz/scant ⅔ cup water
2 tbsp olive oil, plus extra for greasing
100ml/3½fl oz/scant ½ cup chipotle barbecue sauce (see page 113), plus extra to serve

Preheat the oven to 200°C/400°F/ Gas 6.

Place the flour, a pinch of salt and a little black pepper with the cumin, paprika, yeast flakes, oregano, gram flour, onion salt, garlic powder, tahini, tamari and bouillon powder in a large bowl. Add the water and mix thoroughly, then when it's pretty well combined, knead it in the bowl for a further couple of minutes.

Lightly grease a baking pan with olive oil, then transfer the mixture into it and press it down to flatten to about 1cm/½in thick. Use a knife to cut it into slices roughly 2cm/¾in wide and 10cm/4in long.

Place in the oven and bake for about 30 minutes.

Remove the seitan from the oven and transfer to a bowl. Once cool, gently coat in the barbecue sauce and the 2 tablespoons of olive oil, cover with clingfilm (plastic wrap) and leave to marinate in the fridge for at least an hour (but longer if you'd like to). During this time, prepare the grill if cooking outdoors.

When your grill is ready (or use a griddle plate if indoors), grill the marinated seitan slices, turning as needed to get a nice colour on both sides. Serve with a little more barbecue sauce on the side.

YAKITORI SKEWERS

SERVES 4
(MAKES
ABOUT 8
SKEWERS)
V

Yakitori is a Japanese skewered chicken dish; we've just got back from an amazing trip to Japan where we saw it everywhere but never a vegetarian version. Back home, we resolved to find a way we could enjoy its salty, sweet, sticky yumminess and this recipe is the result. They're a brilliant street food-style snack, but they're also great as the protein element in a general barbecue spread or served alongside a rice dish like the jollof pot (see page 29). There are so many vegan 'chicken' options these days but we tend to use the ones from Vivera. It doesn't matter too much which ones you go for, but do try to make sure they're quite big pieces, as anything too shredded won't hold. Smoked tofu also works well if preferred. Remember, you can make the yakitori sauce beforehand to bring with you if it's easier.

8 metal or bamboo skewers

20g/¾oz/3¼ tbsp cornflour (cornstarch)

2 tbsp water

100ml/3½fl oz/scant ½ cup sake

20g/¾oz fresh ginger, peeled and finely chopped

20g/¾oz/1½ tbsp unrefined brown sugar

50ml/1¾oz/3½ tbsp mirin

50ml/1¾oz/3½ tbsp tamari

350g/12oz vegan 'chicken' pieces

6 spring onions (scallions), cut into 2-cm/¾-in lengths

a little vegetable oil, for brushing

1 tbsp sesame seeds, to serve

Prepare your grill if cooking outdoors.

Soak the bamboo skewers (if using) in water as this stops them from burning when they hit the barbecue.

Begin by making the yakitori. Put the cornflour with the water in a small bowl and mix. Place a pot on the barbecue grill – or on the hob (stove) if indoors – and flambé the sake. Add the ginger, sugar, mirin and tamari and quickly bring to the boil, then immediately remove from the heat as you don't want it to reduce too much. Return to the heat when you're ready for the next step and slowly add in a teaspoon at a time of the cornflour mix, whisking continuously, until the sauce has thickened to the consistency of ketchup. You probably won't need all the cornflour mix. Remove from the heat and place to one side.

Assemble the skewers, leaving about 7cm/3in free at one end. We thread on a piece of 'chicken', then a piece of spring onion, then another 'chicken' and so on until the skewer is full. Brush the skewers with a thin layer of vegetable oil.

If cooking outdoors, once your grill is hot, place the skewers onto it and grill until they're nearly cooked on all sides. If cooking indoors, follow the same instructions but use a griddle plate on the hob.

Once the skewers are nearly cooked, brush liberally with the yakitori sauce. Place back on the grill or hob, turning regularly, until they're lovely and charred all over.

Sprinkle over the sesame seeds and serve hot.

MAKES 8
FLATBREADS
V

4g/⅛oz/generous 1 tsp easy bake yeast
1 tbsp white sugar
375ml/13fl oz/1½ cups + 2 tbsp warm water
560g/1¼lb/4 cups strong white bread flour,
plus extra for dusting
salt
2 tbsp olive oil, plus a little extra for
greasing and optional dipping

LAFFA BREAD

We first had this flatbread in Israel and fell in love with it. A bit like pita bread but fluffier and chewier, it's really easy to cook on a fire and great served as part of a barbecue spread. It also works as a standalone dish 'pizza' style (see opposite – you can also just follow the first part of that recipe to get amazing barbecued garlic bread).

Mix together the yeast, sugar and warm water in a bowl and leave to one side for about 10 minutes.

Put the flour and a pinch of salt in a large bowl. Stir in the prepared yeast mixture and then the olive oil.

Tip the dough out onto a floured surface and knead for about 5–10 minutes until smooth. You can always add a little more flour as you go if it gets too sticky. Place the dough back in the big bowl, cover with clingfilm (plastic wrap) and poke a few small holes in the film to allow it to breath. Cover with a damp cloth and leave in a warm spot (quite near to the campfire if outdoors) for about an hour until risen.

Remove the cloth and clingfilm and gently punch the dough to remove the air. Then transfer back to a floured surface and gently roll into a cylinder. Divide into 8 pieces, then roll into balls and transfer onto a greased baking sheet or tray. Cover again with clingfilm and return to a warm place for about a further 10 minutes while you prepare the grill if you're cooking outdoors. Use a griddle plate on the hob (stove) if you're indoors.

On the floured surface (make sure you keep the surface well floured throughout), roll each portion until it's about 4mm/¼in thick. Use a spatula to transfer each bread to the hot grill and chargrill until bubbles start to appear. Lift a little of the bread with a spatula to check it's evenly cooked on the bottom, then flip and do the other side.

Delicious served hot with a generous pinch of salt and a little olive oil to dip.

LAFFA BREAD 'PIZZA'

6 tbsp olive oil, plus 2 tbsp for the onions, and extra for drizzling (optional)

6 garlic cloves, crushed

2 sprigs rosemary, finely chopped

salt and black pepper

1 batch laffa bread dough in 8 pieces (see opposite)

1 onion, chopped

200g/7oz picked kale, chopped

360g/12¾oz/1½ cups soft cheese

Laffa bread (see opposite) is a brilliant and easy bread to make and enjoy at a barbecue, but this recipe turns it into a meal in itself. You can either serve this like a pizza, or you could also roll it up into wraps – and definitely feel free to experiment with toppings! Alternatively, just follow the first part for irresistible garlic bread.

Prepare the grill if cooking outdoors.

While the grill is heating up (or use a griddle plate if you're cooking indoors), make the garlic mixture by combining the 6 tablespoons of olive oil, the garlic, rosemary and a generous pinch of salt and black pepper in a bowl. This is all you need if you're just making garlic bread: simply spread a generous amount of it onto each rolled-out laffa dough and then transfer to the grill using a spatula to make it easier. Grill the non-garlic side first until it starts to bubble, check the underside is nicely chargrilled by lifting it up with your spatula and if it is, flip it over to chargrill the garlic side for a minute or two. You want to get some colour but be careful it doesn't burn and check again with the spatula to see when it's ready. Season to taste and drizzle over a touch more olive oil if desired.

If you're making the 'pizza', before cooking the bread, place a frying pan or skillet on the grill or hob (stove) and heat the 2 tablespoons of olive oil. Add the onions with some salt and black pepper and sauté for about 5 minutes until they start to caramelize. Add all the kale and a splash of water and continue to cook for about 3 minutes until the kale is wilted. Adjust the seasoning to taste and place to one side.

Grill the breads in batches with the garlic mixture as above and when they're ready, spread an eighth of the soft cheese onto the garlic side of each bread and then top with a handful of the kale mix.

ROSEMARY SWEET POTATO 'CHIPS'

SERVES 2–4
AS PART OF
A MEAL
V / WF / GF

50ml/1¾fl oz/3½ tbsp olive oil
700g/1lb 9oz sweet potatoes, skins on and thinly sliced, ideally on a mandoline
salt and black pepper
2 sprigs rosemary, finely chopped

A mandoline is a great piece of kit and, although a knife will certainly do, the key here is to get beautifully thin, uniform slices. We highly recommend getting a mandoline (particularly a Benriner), but please do use the safety guard! Kids love 'chips' and they are excellent dipped in either our homemade ketchup (see page 121) or barbecue sauce (see page 113).

Prepare the grill if cooking outdoors. Put the olive oil in a large bowl, add the sweet potato slices and move them around so they're lightly coated in the oil. Add a couple of pinches of salt and a generous twist of black pepper along with the rosemary and mix by hand until the slices are evenly covered.

When your grill is ready, cook the slices in batches, turning as needed to get good colour on both sides.

If cooking indoors, place the slices on a griddle plate on the hob (stove) over a medium-high heat and prepare in the same way as outdoors. Serve hot!

EMBER & ASH

BURNT LEEK VINAIGRETTE

SERVES 4
AS A SIDE
V / WF / GF

4 leeks
1 tsp Dijon mustard
2 tbsp white wine vinegar
3 tbsp olive oil
1 shallot, finely chopped
1 tbsp capers
10g/⅓ oz parsley, chopped
salt and black pepper

This is a wonderful and simple way to prepare leeks and makes a great side dish at a veggie barbecue. You can either enjoy it straightaway or you can also make it ahead of time and keep it in the fridge overnight to further intensify the flavours.

Prepare the embers (see page 10) and then place the leeks directly into them. Allow the leeks to cook, turning frequently, until they're well charred on all sides and tender when poked with a skewer. (Don't worry about them becoming blackened and covered in ashes as you'll remove the outer layers later on.) Alternatively, you can char the leeks on a grill, or on a super-hot griddle plate on the hob (stove) if cooking indoors.

While the leeks are cooking, quickly prepare the vinaigrette by whisking together the mustard, vinegar and olive oil in a bowl. Place to one side.

Allow the cooked leeks to cool slightly, then peel off the burnt outer layers and discard (don't worry about being too fanatical, as any little burnt bits left on will enhance the flavour). Slice the leeks in half lengthways and arrange on a serving platter, then pour over the vinaigrette and top with the shallots, capers and parsley. Season to taste with a little salt and black pepper.

EMBER-ROASTED VEGETABLE PLATE

SERVES 2
VO / WF / GF

Rescoldo, or cooking in the embers and ashes, is a fantastic and very visually appealing way to prepare and celebrate vegetables in their purest form. Take the ingredients in this recipe as a suggestion only; really you can substitute our ideas for anything you fancy or have to hand: pumpkins, aubergines, peppers, sweetcorn, potatoes, squashes, onions ... the list goes on. We serve this with some of our kalamata tapenade and an optional block of feta cheese.

2 aubergines (eggplants)
2 red peppers
2 onions
2 sweet potatoes
1 butternut squash
100g/3½oz rocket (arugula)
1 block feta cheese (optional)
1 batch kalamata tapenade (see page 109)

Prepare the embers (see page 10) and then bury all the vegetables directly into the embers and ashes, making sure they are fully covered. Allow them to roast for at least 10 minutes and then spread the embers so you can check on progress. Use tongs to turn the vegetables and insert a skewer to see whether the potatoes and squash are ready. If you need to roast for longer, replace the embers and continue to cook until each element is ready.

Carefully dig the vegetables out when they're ready and wipe off the embers and ashes. Remove the outer layers of the onions and cut them in half; peel, deseed and core the peppers and then slice lengthways; slice the aubergine lengthways; and cut the potatoes and squash into chunks.

Arrange the rocket on a platter and then add all the vegetables along with the slab of feta, if using. Top generously with the tapenade.

Vegan option Omit the feta cheese.

EMBER-ROASTED SMOKED ONIONS

MAKES
6 ONIONS
V / WF / GF

6 onions,
100g/3½oz (approx) woodchips of choice,
soaked in water

These onions are a really versatile ingredient to have to hand at a barbecue. They're great as a topping for burgers, skewers or hot dog type things but are also excellent in a salad or chopped and used to add a smoky flavour to any dish. Woodchips are easy to find online or in garden centres or some cookery shops. We tend to go for hickory, oak or mesquite but whatever takes your fancy will be perfect.

This technique works best in a kettle style barbecue so you can close the lid to maximise the smoky flavour, but you can also do it in the embers of an open fire.

Prepare the embers and then place the onions directly on top of them. After about 10 minutes of roasting, scatter the woodchips around the onions as close as you can to them. Close the lid if you're using a kettle style barbecue and continue to roast for around a further 10 minutes until they're soft on the inside and have a good charred colour on the outside. Throughout this roasting time, rotate every 5 minutes or so to prevent complete burning. You do however want to allow them to really char on the outside.

Remove from the kettle and leave to cool before removing the charred outer skin layers.

EMBER-BAKED SWEET POTATOES WITH BLACK BEANS & SOUR CREAM

SERVES 4
VO / WF / GF

4 sweet potatoes
2 tbsp olive oil, plus extra for drizzling
salt
1 onion, sliced
2 garlic cloves, sliced
½ tsp ground cumin
½ tsp ground cinnamon
½ tsp hot smoked paprika
black pepper
1 x 400-g/14-oz can black beans, drained and rinsed
200ml/7fl oz/scant 1 cup water
150g/5½oz/scant ⅔ cup sour cream
8 sprigs coriander (cilantro), picked

This is one of our favourite simple camping dishes and the potatoes are best enjoyed still in their foil, so it saves on dishes too! It's satisfying as it is, but also lovely with some avocado or tomato salsa on the side. If you're going to be short on time, it's also an option to cook the potatoes indoors and then just heat them up on the fire.

Prepare the embers (see page 10) or preheat the oven to 200°C/400°F/Gas 6. Spike the sweet potatoes a few times with a fork (this will stop them exploding in the fire!) and then place each potato onto a large piece of foil. Drizzle a little olive oil onto each potato and then rub it all over the skin. Give each potato a pinch of salt and then wrap in the foil. If cooking outdoors, place in the embers, making sure each potato is fully covered, and bake for somewhere between 45 minutes and 1 hour 15 minutes. Add more embers if needed as the potatoes cook to ensure there's enough heat. Check if they're ready by opening one of the packages and poking with a knife to see if they're soft all the way through. If cooking indoors, place the potatoes in the oven and bake for around 45 minutes until soft inside.

While the potatoes are baking, place a skillet over your chosen outdoor heat source or over a medium heat if using the hob (stove). Heat the 2 tablespoons of olive oil, then add the onion slices and a pinch of salt and sauté for about 3 minutes, moving them around occasionally. Add the garlic and continue to sauté for a further 2 minutes before mixing in the cumin, cinnamon, smoked paprika and a little black pepper. Continue to cook for another couple of minutes or so before adding in the black beans. Stir in the water and allow to cook out for about 5–7 minutes, stirring occasionally, until the mixture is fairly dried out. Add a little more salt and black pepper if needed.

Remove the potatoes from the embers when they're ready, open the foil, cut a hole in each potato and tear a little to open up. Drizzle in a dash more olive oil and spoon over some of the black bean mixture. Add a generous dollop of sour cream and a sprinkling of coriander leaves.

Vegan option Omit the sour cream or use a plant-based alternative.

EMBER-ROASTED PUMPKIN TAGINE

SERVES 4
VO / WF / GF
(IF USING AN
ALTERNATIVE TO
COUSCOUS)

1 medium pumpkin (about 2kg/4½lb)

salt

45g/1½oz/3 tbsp butter

4 bay leaves

1 large onion, sliced

1 tbsp olive oil, plus a little extra

3 garlic cloves, crushed

½ tsp ground cumin

¼ tsp ground coriander

1 x 400-g/14-oz can chopped tomatoes

1 tbsp honey

1 tbsp rose harissa

100g/3½oz/¾ cup chopped dried apricots

30g/1oz/¼ cup raisins

1 x 400-g/14-oz can chickpeas

skin of 1 preserved lemon, thinly sliced

200ml/7fl oz/scant 1 cup water

5 carrots, chopped

black pepper

250g/9oz/generous 1 cup labneh or natural yogurt

45g/1½oz/½ cup flaked (sliced) almonds, toasted

8 sprigs coriander (cilantro), picked

500g/1lb 2oz/3 cups couscous or alternative, cooked

This is such a dramatic addition to a barbecue table! It's probably best to par-roast the pumpkin in advance to take with you and then finish it off in the embers, but you could in theory do the whole thing in the embers, it would just take a long time and need a lot of them! If you're going to do that, just place the pumpkin directly in the embers, cover it completely and roast until it feels tender all over when poked with a skewer.

If cooking indoors, preheat the oven to 190°C/375°F/Gas 5. If outdoors, prepare the embers (see page 10).

Slice off the top of the pumpkin, keeping the stem intact, and scrape out all the fibrous bits and the seeds from both parts. Put a couple of pinches of salt, the butter and 2 bay leaves into the main cavity, cover with the top, transfer to a roasting pan and bake for about 60 minutes. It's ready when it seems a little tender but still firm when poked with a skewer. If you're not going to use the embers, then cook for a little longer until fully tender. If it starts to get too much colour, loosely cover with foil.

In a Dutch oven or large pot, either over the fire or on the hob (stove), sauté the onion in the olive oil for a couple of minutes until translucent. Add the garlic, cumin and coriander and a dash more olive oil if necessary and continue to cook for a further couple of minutes, stirring as needed. Add the tomatoes, remaining bay leaves, honey, harissa, apricots, raisins, chickpeas, preserved lemon, water, carrots and a generous pinch of salt and black pepper, mix well and continue to cook (if on the hob, on a low-medium heat) for about 20–25 minutes, stirring regularly. Season again to taste and place to one side.

When the pumpkin is ready, remove and discard any liquid that might have collected in the cavity (or use it as part of the water to cook the couscous in if you haven't already). Scoop the warm tagine mix into the pumpkin (any extra can just be served on the side) and carefully cover with the pumpkin lid. Either serve as it is if you're indoors and have cooked it for longer or, if outdoors, return it to the embers for around 15 minutes until the pumpkin is tender and the tagine hot. Transfer to a large serving dish.

Have the labneh or yogurt, flaked almonds, coriander and couscous ready on the side and then open up the pumpkin with a flourish. It looks fantastic steaming away! Scoop portions of the tagine out, making sure you scoop some of the pumpkin from the sides too.

Vegan option Use a plant-based spread instead of butter and substitute a plant-based yogurt. Replace the honey with brown sugar.

EMBER-BAKED CINNAMON SPICED APPLES

MAKES 4
VO / WF / GF

4 cooking apples, cored and with a line
scored around the centre

40g/1½oz/3¼ tbsp unrefined brown sugar

40g/1½oz/¼ cup raisins

1 tsp ground cinnamon

pinch of ground nutmeg

35g/1¼oz/2½ tbsp butter

2 tbsp honey

4 cloves

crème fraîche or Greek yogurt, to serve

This is a very straightforward camping dessert, perfect for warming and comforting on a chilly evening outdoors. If you're not sure about using the embers, it can also be done on the grill or at home in the oven.

If cooking indoors, preheat the oven to 180°C/350°F/Gas 4. If outdoors, prepare the embers (see page 10).

Place the apples into an ovenproof dish if indoors, or onto individual pieces of foil big enough to ultimately wrap them in, if cooking outdoors.

Mix together the sugar, raisins, cinnamon and nutmeg in a bowl and then place equal amounts of this mixture into the centre of each apple. Stuff an equal amount of the butter and then the honey into each centre, then press a clove into the side of each apple too.

If indoors, spoon 2 tablespoons of water over the apples and then bake in the oven for 30–45 minutes until tender. If outdoors, wrap the apples in the foil and place them directly in the embers of the fire (or on the grill) for about 20–30 minutes (turning a couple of times at least if on the grill), poking with a small knife to check when they're tender. In any case, it doesn't matter if they start to collapse a bit.

Remove the cloves and serve hot with crème fraîche or yogurt.

Vegan option Omit the honey and use plant-based alternatives for the butter and crème fraîche or yogurt.

SALADS

SERVES 2–4
V / WF / GF

ISRAELI SALAD

This simple salad is freshness in a bowl and immediately takes us back to the Middle Eastern sun. It's very straightforward but is lovely to include on a barbecue table or as part of a wrap. We've used it in our sabich sandwich recipe (see page 56).

Simply mix together the cucumber, tomatoes, mint, parsley, lemon juice and olive oil in a large bowl. Season to taste with salt and black pepper and serve.

¼ cucumber, deseeded and diced
10 cherry tomatoes, diced
1 tbsp chopped mint
2 tbsp chopped flat-leaf parsley
2 tsp lemon juice
1 tsp olive oil
salt and black pepper

CRÈME FRAÎCHE POTATO SALAD

SERVES 4
AS A SIDE
WF / GF

750g/1lb 10oz new potatoes, boiled
200g/7oz/scant 1 cup crème fraîche
salt and black pepper
2 spring onions (scallions), thinly sliced

It's not a barbecue without a potato salad and this is an incredibly easy one to quickly put together. The crème fraîche is a delicious way to dress the salad and it also makes it a little less heavy; ideal if you've got lots of other yummy things to tuck into, too!

When the potatoes are cool, cut them in half and place in a large bowl. Mix in the crème fraîche and some salt and black pepper, then sprinkle the spring onions over the top to serve.

WATERMELON & GRILLED HALLOUMI SALAD WITH LEMON VINAIGRETTE & MINT

SERVES 2–4
WF / GF

We've served halloumi with our Buddha bowls for nearly 10 years, so have a longstanding relationship with our Cypriot halloumi supplier! We were bowled over when he one day let us try some of the packed lunch his wife had made for him of grilled halloumi and watermelon. It's a winning combination that really tastes of summer!

2 tbsp lemon juice

1 tbsp olive oil

salt and black pepper

250g/9oz halloumi, cut into 1-cm/½-in thick slices

½ small watermelon, quartered and cut into 1-cm/½-in thick slices

5g/⅛oz mint leaves, roughly chopped

Begin by making the simple vinaigrette. In a small bowl, use a fork to whisk together the lemon juice and olive oil and season to taste with salt and black pepper.

Grill the halloumi slices until they're nice and golden on both sides (you can use a griddle plate on the hob/stove if you're cooking indoors). Place in a large bowl along with the watermelon slices, then pour over the vinaigrette and sprinkle over the chopped mint. Top with a little extra black pepper.

For the tofu

1 tbsp olive oil

450g/1lb braised tofu, drained

1 batch bulgogi marinade (see page 114)

10g/⅓oz sesame seeds

For the rice

30ml/1fl oz/2 tbsp mirin

30ml/1fl oz/2 tbsp brown rice vinegar

pinch of salt

250g/9oz/1⅓ cups short-grain
brown rice, cooked

For the rest

4–6 nori sheets

1 carrot, thinly sliced

½ cucumber, thinly sliced

½ red pepper, thinly sliced

1 red apple, cored and quartered,
then finely sliced (or Asian pear
if you can find it)

50g/¾oz pickled daikon, cut into batons
(optional)

1 spring onion (scallion), top and tailed
and thinly sliced

½ batch oi kimchi (see page 107), to serve
(optional)

BRAISED TOFU BULGOGI KIMBAP ROLLS

SERVES 4
V / WF / GF

This braised tofu bulgogi is one of our favourite things to prepare for a barbecue and it's great in these kimbap rolls. We use Marigold braised tofu, which comes in a tin and is easily found in most health food shops or online.

You'll need a sushi mat to form this into rolls, but if you don't have one, you can also serve it as a salad, with the nori sheets cut into thin strips like a sprinkle. Or cut the nori into large triangles, form a cone, wet one side to seal and then simply stuff it with the fillings.

This is delicious served with some of our oi kimchi, or any other kimchi, and some boiled eggs on the side work well too if you're not vegan.

Heat the olive oil for the tofu in a skillet or frying pan over a medium heat. Add the braised tofu and fry for about 5 minutes until it becomes nice and dry. Break it down as you go by crushing it a bit with a wooden spoon or spatula. Add 150ml/5fl oz/scant ⅔ cup of the bulgogi marinade and keep on the heat, stirring regularly, until the mixture is once again mostly dried out and resembles pulled meat. Stir in the sesame seeds, then remove from the heat and leave to one side.

For the rice, add the mirin, brown rice vinegar and salt to the cooked rice

(ideally while it's still hot) and mix well. Transfer to a plate, cover with a clean damp tea towel and leave to cool.

Place the shiny side of a nori sheet down on your sushi mat. Spread about 170g/6oz of the rice mixture onto the nori sheet leaving a strip about 5cm/2in at one end uncovered. Keep a bowl of cold water close by to stop your hands from getting too sticky. In the middle, layer some of the carrot, cucumber, red pepper, apple, daikon and spring onion and top with braised bulgogi tofu, but not so much that you won't be able to roll

your kimbap. Lightly wet the empty strip with your finger and, using the mat, roll the kimbap towards the empty strip, which will serve to stick it together. Cut the roll in half across and repeat to get 8 slices.

Repeat this process for as many times as you have ingredients, we usually get between 4 and 6 complete rolls from this amount.

Serve with any extra bulgogi marinade as a dipping sauce, and some oi kimchi on the side, if you like.

BURNT CAULIFLOWER SALAD WITH TAHINI YOGURT & POMEGRANATE

SERVES 2–4
WF / GF

This is a take on a dish we devoured on our first night in Tel Aviv. It's a winner because it uses pretty much all of our favourite ingredients from that part of the world in one flavour-packed dish. It's great as it is, but it can also be piled up on top of a laffa bread (see page 72) or other flatbread, and you can add sliced boiled egg too, if you feel like it. If you wanted to prepare this all outdoors, you could alternatively barbecue buttered slices of cauliflower and then baste them with the harissa mix towards the end of the cooking time.

pinch of salt
1 cauliflower, cut into florets
50g/1¾oz/3½ tbsp butter
1 garlic clove, chopped
½ tsp sumac
½ tsp cumin seeds, toasted
salt and black pepper
2 tsp harissa
1½ tbsp tahini
4 tbsp natural yogurt
1 tbsp olive oil
juice and zest of ¼ lemon
1 tbsp pomegranate molasses
seeds of ½ pomegranate
15g/½oz parsley, roughly chopped
10g/⅓oz mint leaves, roughly chopped
20g/¾oz/¼ cup flaked (sliced) almonds, toasted

Preheat the oven to 240°C/475°F/Gas 8.

Bring a large pan of water to the boil with a good pinch of salt and blanch the cauliflower florets for 5 minutes. Drain and place to one side.

Melt the butter in a skillet or ovenproof frying pan and add the blanched florets. Coat them with the butter, then pour out 2 teaspoons of the butter and place it to one side. Transfer the buttered cauliflower florets to the oven and roast for about 10–15 minutes until they have taken on some colour. Move them around a couple of times during cooking.

Meanwhile, using a pestle and mortar, grind together the garlic, sumac and toasted cumin seeds along with a little black pepper. Add the harissa and continue to grind. Stir in the reserved melted butter from earlier and tip into a bowl.

Add the roasted cauliflower to the bowl, stir well to coat in the spice mix, then return to the pan and roast for a further 10–15 minutes until it really starts to blacken.

While the cauliflower is roasting, make the dressing by mixing the tahini, yogurt, olive oil and lemon juice and zest together in a bowl.

When everything is ready, place the cauliflower in a serving bowl, drizzle over any buttery mixture that's left in the skillet and then add the tahini dressing to taste. Top with the pomegranate molasses, pomegranate seeds, parsley, mint and toasted almonds, and season with a little salt and pepper, if needed.

RAINBOW SLAW

SERVES 4
AS A SIDE
V / WF / GF

¼ white cabbage (about 400g/14oz), finely sliced

¼ red cabbage (about 400g/14oz), finely sliced

½ white onion, finely sliced

2 carrots, grated

¼ bunch mint, roughly chopped

2 spring onions (scallions), thinly sliced

2–3 tbsp mixed seeds (such as sesame, sunflower, poppy, flax)

75ml/2½fl oz/5 tbsp brown rice vinegar

50ml/1¾fl oz/3½ tbsp mirin

1 tsp toasted sesame oil

2 handfuls mixed sprouts

This is lovely to have on a barbecue table to enjoy with things like pulled jackfruit (see page 38) or sticky tempeh 'ribs' (see page 62). You can buy sprouts from health food shops or some supermarkets, or it's also very easy to sprout your own. We try to get them into lots of our dishes, as they're super nutritious!

Combine all the vegetables (except the sprouts) and seeds in a bowl.

In a separate bowl, mix together the rice vinegar, mirin and sesame oil, then pour this over the vegetables and mix to combine. Top with a couple of handfuls of mixed sprouts just before serving.

COWBOY CAVIAR

SERVES 4
V / WF / GF

Also known as Texas caviar, this is a classic American party dish from the 1940s. Loaded with vegetables and protein-packed beans, it's so fresh and healthy but also really substantial. We love to serve a big bowl of it almost like an oversized salsa, with lots of corn tortilla chips on the side.

1 small red onion, diced

1 red pepper, diced

1 green pepper diced

270g/9½oz/1½ cups cherry tomatoes, diced

45g/1½oz pickled jalapeño chillies, diced

200g/7oz canned sweetcorn, drained

1 x 400-g/14-oz can black-eyed beans (peas), drained and rinsed

1 x 400-g/14-oz can black beans, drained and rinsed

1 avocado, peeled, pitted and diced

30g/1oz coriander (cilantro), roughly chopped

For the dressing

2 tbsp red wine vinegar

juice of 1 lime

1 tsp unrefined brown sugar

½ tsp red chilli flakes

½ tsp ground cumin

½ garlic clove, crushed

50ml/1¾fl oz/3½ tbsp olive oil

salt and black pepper

1 bag corn tortilla chips, to serve

Place the red onion, red and green peppers, cherry tomatoes, jalapeños, sweetcorn, black-eyed beans, black beans, avocado and coriander in a large bowl and gently mix so they're well combined.

Make the dressing by mixing together the red wine vinegar, lime juice, brown sugar, chilli flakes, cumin, garlic, olive oil and some salt and pepper to taste.

Pour the dressing over the salad and gently mix it through so it is thoroughly combined.

Serve with tortilla chips.

DEVILLED EGGS

MAKES 12
WF / GF

These retro beauties are a lovely thing to have on the table at a summer barbecue, or at any party really! The gherkin liquid is just the pickling liquid from a jar of gherkins and isn't vital, but it does add a rather delicious sweet piquancy to the eggs. You can make this more of a salad by placing the eggs on a bed of little gem lettuce.

6 eggs, hard boiled (for about 12 minutes), peeled and cut in half lengthways
1 tsp Dijon mustard
4 tbsp mayonnaise
1 tsp white wine vinegar
1 tsp gherkin pickling liquid
salt and black pepper
smoked paprika, to sprinkle

Gently remove the yolks from the egg halves using a teaspoon. Finely grate them into a bowl before adding the mustard, mayonnaise, white wine vinegar, gherkin liquid and a little salt and black pepper to taste. Mix thoroughly. If the mixture is at all lumpy you can push it through a strainer. Fill each of the egg white halves with the yolk mixture and top with a pinch of smoked paprika, salt and a little more cracked black pepper.

SAUCES & SIDES

OI KIMCHI

MAKES ABOUT
1KG/2¼LB
VO / WF / GF

It's great to have a jar of this cucumber kimchi around as it's such an easy way to add freshness and a bit of spice and crunch to all kinds of dishes. Baby cucumbers have a lovely flavour but normal ones are also fine if you can't track the mini ones down. Unlike traditional kimchi, this can be enjoyed after just three hours, although you can also leave it overnight in the fridge. It is, however, best to try and eat it within a day.

It's quite spicy but you can reduce (or increase!) the amount of chilli flakes depending on your preference.

1kg/2lb 4oz baby cucumbers, cut into batons
1 small shallot, finely sliced
1 tbsp salt
2 garlic cloves, chopped
8g/¼oz fresh ginger, peeled and roughly chopped
1 tbsp red chilli flakes
¼ red apple, grated
1 tbsp honey
1 tbsp tamari

Place the cucumber batons and sliced shallots in a large bowl. Add the salt and mix by hand to evenly distribute. Leave to one side for at least 10 minutes.

Place the garlic and ginger in a pestle and mortar and begin to grind. Add the chilli flakes and continue to grind before adding the apple, honey and tamari and grinding until it becomes a coarse paste.

Drain any excess water from the cucumbers and shallots and then use a clean tea towel or paper towels to dry them off a bit. Return the to the bowl and spoon over the chilli paste. Mix thoroughly by hand, cover and leave in a cool place for about 3 hours. If not using immediately, you can transfer to a sterilized jar (see page 115) and store in the fridge overnight.

Vegan option Use brown sugar in place of the honey.

KALAMATA TAPENADE

MAKES ABOUT
200G/7OZ
V / WF / GF

100g/3½oz/1 cup pitted kalamata olives, finely chopped
2 tbsp capers, finely chopped
1 tsp lemon zest
1 tbsp lemon juice
1 tsp dried oregano
100ml/3½fl oz/scant ½ cup olive oil
pinch of black pepper

You can't beat a freshly made tapenade for strong, zingy flavours that really pop. It's wonderful spooned over a slab of feta or some steaming new potatoes, but it's also an ideal accompaniment to our ember-roasted vegetable plate (see page 80). The tapenade is best eaten immediately, but it does also keep well for about a week in the fridge.

Mix all the ingredients together in a bowl until well combined.

CHIMICHURRI

MAKES ABOUT
100G/3½OZ
V / WF / GF

Originating in Argentina and Uruguay, chimichurri is an uncooked sauce often used as a marinade for grilled meat. You can use it in this way with any meat substitutes you enjoy having on the barbecue, but it is also wonderful as a condiment or drizzled over grilled or ember-roasted vegetables (see page 80). Another thing we love to do is add a spoonful to natural yogurt to make a delicious dip!

It's meant to be seriously garlicky, and we don't disappoint in that regard here, but you can reduce to one clove if you're not so keen or have a hot date lined up. It can, of course, be prepared in a food processor but we like to make it using a pestle and mortar, especially when we're outdoors

salt
2 garlic cloves, chopped
30g/1oz parsley, roughly chopped
1 tsp dried oregano
½ tsp red chilli flakes
2 tbsp red wine vinegar
4 tbsp olive oil

Place a generous pinch of salt into your mortar. Add the garlic cloves and crush thoroughly. Add the parsley, oregano, chilli flakes and red wine vinegar and grind until it all begins to break down. Add the olive oil and continue to grind until you have a wet, well-combined yet still rough mixture.

CHIPOTLE BARBECUE SAUCE

MAKES ABOUT
400ML/14FL OZ/
1¾ CUPS
V / WF / GF

It isn't a barbecue without some barbecue sauce and this is something we always have to hand; the addition of chipotle giving it a little bit of a kick. It also works as a great marinade for veggies or for jackfruit (see page 38), as well as for soya or seitan products (see page 70).

1 tbsp olive oil

3 garlic cloves, crushed

1 small onion, chopped

2 tbsp chopped thyme

1 tbsp molasses

1 chipotle chilli, soaked in hot water for about 15 minutes until soft, drained and chopped

30ml/1fl oz/2 tbsp rum

2 tsp red wine vinegar

30ml/1fl oz/2 tbsp tamari

300ml/10½fl oz/generous 1¼ cups ketchup

Salt and pepper

1 x 400-ml/14-fl oz/1¾-cup bottle or jar, sterilized

Heat the oil in a pan and sauté the garlic, onion and thyme for 2 minutes before adding the molasses and softened chipotle. Allow the mixture to caramelize for a minute, then add the rum, vinegar and tamari and cook for a further 2 minutes.

Add the ketchup and a touch of salt and pepper and mix thoroughly. Bring the sauce to the boil, then turn down the heat and simmer for 10–15 minutes, stirring occasionally.

Allow to cool, then transfer to your sterilized bottle or jar to store in the fridge.

To sterilize your jar Bring a large pan of water to the boil. Remove from the heat and, using tongs, carefully lower the jar and lid into the water. Submerge the head of the tongs as well. Leave everything for 5 minutes then lift the jar out of the water using the same tongs and allow to air dry.

BULGOGI MARINADE

MAKES
200ML/7FL OZ/
SCANT 1 CUP
V / WF / GF

80ml/2½fl oz/5 tbsp tamari
80ml/2½fl oz/5 tbsp mirin
30g/1oz/2½ tbsp unrefined brown sugar
4g/⅛oz/1 tbsp red chilli flakes
4 garlic cloves
1 tsp toasted sesame oil

Bulgogi translates as 'fire-meat', so obviously in a veggie book this isn't an authentic bulgogi. But the marinade used for bulgogi is such a handy thing to have around at a veggie barbecue. We use it with our braised tofu kimbap (see page 97), but it's also great as a general marinade or sauce and works really well with jackfruit or soya or seitan products. Double the chilli flakes if you'd like it authentically spicy!

Place all the ingredients into a blender and blend until smooth.

PICKLED RED CHILLIES

MAKES
ABOUT
350G/12OZ
V / WF / GF

100ml/3½fl oz/scant ½ cup apple
cider vinegar
100ml/3½fl oz/scant ½ cup water
1 bay leaf
30g/1oz/2½ tbsp unrefined brown sugar
1 tsp coriander seeds
½ tsp ground turmeric
½ tsp cumin seeds
salt and black pepper
5 long red chillies, sliced
1 x 400-ml/14-fl oz/1¾-cup jar, sterilized

We usually have lots of red chillies leftover from making kimchi for our Buddha bowls and we love to pickle them so they don't go to waste. Ideal for quickly adding a bit of tangy heat to any dish, you'll need a jar that can hold about 400ml/14fl oz/1¾ cups. You can also try substituting the sliced red chillies for whole habaneros, as our friend Henning from The Taco Truck showed us. They make a snack that certainly wakes you up if you're feeling a bit sluggish!

Place the vinegar, water, bay leaf, sugar, coriander seeds, turmeric and cumin seeds into a pan and bring to the boil so the sugar dissolves. Add a pinch of salt and black pepper and leave to one side.

Place the sliced red chilli into your sterilized pickling jar and then pour in the hot pickling liquor. Set aside to cool with the lid off and once it's cool, seal and transfer to the fridge. It will be ready in a couple of days and should last at least a couple of weeks.

To sterilize your jar Bring a large pan of water to the boil. Remove from the heat and, using tongs, carefully lower the jar and lid into the water. Submerge the head of the tongs as well. Leave everything for 5 minutes then lift the jar out of the water using the same tongs and allow to air dry.

MAKES ABOUT
2.5KG/5½LB
V / WF / GF

1 large jar (about 2 litres/70fl oz), sterilized

750g/1lb 10oz turnips, peeled and cut into batons roughly 1cm/½in wide

200g/7oz beetroot, peeled and sliced

2 bay leaves

750ml/26fl oz/3¼ cups water

200ml/7fl oz/scant 1 cup white wine vinegar

2 garlic cloves

3 tbsp salt

PICKLED TURNIPS

These are a great thing to have around, not only because they're delicious but because the addition of beetroot also turns them the kind of neon pink that you can't believe is natural and that will make any dish pop!

In your sterilized jar, layer the turnip batons and beetroot slices and top with the bay leaves.

In a bowl, whisk the water, vinegar, garlic and salt until all the salt has dissolved.

Pour enough of the vinegar mixture over the turnips and beetroot so they're fully covered and then seal the jar and place in the fridge. It usually takes about a week for them to be ready.

To sterilize your jar Bring a large pan of water to the boil. Remove from the heat and, using tongs, carefully lower the jar and lid into the water. Submerge the head of the tongs as well. Leave everything for 5 minutes then lift the jar out of the water using the same tongs and allow to air dry.

MIXED VEGETABLE PICKLES

MAKES A
1-LITRE/
35-FL OZ JAR
V / WF / GF

A jar of mixed pickles is an excellent way to liven up an outdoor feast. And a great way to use up any unwanted vegetables. The cabbage needs salting to pickle properly, but all the other vegetables can be substituted for whatever you fancy or have going spare.

1-litre/35-fl oz/4¼-cup Kilner jar, sterilized
300g/10½oz white cabbage, sliced
1 tbsp salt, plus a pinch
1 carrot, peeled and cut into batons
85g/3oz cucumber, cut into wedges
70g/2½oz cauliflower, broken into small florets
1 garlic clove
1 long red chilli, halved
½ tsp ground turmeric
180ml/6fl oz/¾ cup apple cider vinegar
360ml/12½fl oz/generous 1½ cups water
50g/1¾oz/¼ cup unrefined brown sugar
½ tsp mustard seeds
½ tsp coriander seeds
1 bay leaf

Place the cabbage in a mixing bowl along with the salt, mix well by hand and then leave to one side for about 30 minutes.

After the 30 minutes, transfer the cabbage to a colander to drain and then weigh it down in the colander using a suitably sized bowl filled with water. Leave to one side for a further 1–2 hours and then rinse the cabbage to remove the salt.

Place the cabbage, carrot, cucumber, cauliflower, garlic, red chilli and turmeric in your sterilized Kilner jar.

Make the pickling liquor by placing the apple cider vinegar, water, brown sugar, mustard seeds, coriander seeds

and a pinch of salt in a pan. Bring it to the boil, stirring occasionally until the sugar is dissolved.

Pour as much as you can of the liquor over the vegetables in the jar, add the bay leaf and allow to fully cool before sealing with the lid and transferring to the fridge. They should be ready to eat after 2–3 days and should keep for around a month.

To sterilize your jar Bring a large pan of water to the boil. Remove from the heat and, using tongs, carefully lower the jar and lid into the water. Submerge the head of the tongs as well. Leave everything for 5 minutes then lift the jar out of the water using the same tongs and allow to air dry.

ROASTED TOMATO KETCHUP

MAKES ABOUT 800ML/28FL OZ
V / WF / GF

You can't have a barbecue without some ketchup and to make your own, and to elevate the flavour by roasting the tomatoes, is an excellent barbecue coup. In an ideal world, they'd be fire roasted but if you're making it indoors, roasted in the oven is delicious too. It's actually super easy and keeps for at least a week in a sealed container in the fridge, so it can be made well ahead of time.

1kg/2lb 4oz plum tomatoes, halved
4 tbsp olive oil
salt and black pepper
1 tbsp dried thyme
2 small onions, chopped
3 garlic cloves, crushed
2 tbsp tomato purée (tomato paste)
½ tsp garlic powder
2 pinches of onion salt
½ tsp ground allspice
½ tsp ground cinnamon
3 cloves
3 bay leaves
1 tsp mustard seeds
75g/2¾oz/6 tbsp unrefined brown sugar
100ml/3½fl oz/scant ½ cup apple cider vinegar
pinch of red chilli flakes

If cooking outdoors, prepare your grill, then brush the tomatoes with 2 tablespoons of the olive oil and sprinkle with a little salt and black pepper and 1 teaspoon of the thyme. Grill until they're just beginning to blacken on all sides.

If cooking indoors, preheat the oven to 220°C/425°F/Gas 7 and place the tomatoes in a baking dish or baking pan lined with greaseproof (wax) paper. Brush the tomatoes with 2 tablespoons of the olive oil and sprinkle with a little salt and black pepper and 1 teaspoon of the thyme (as above). Roast for around 40 minutes until they have lots of colour.

Meanwhile, heat the remaining 2 tablespoons of olive oil in a pan over a medium heat, add the onions and sauté for about 3–5 minutes until translucent. Turn the heat to low, then mix in the garlic, the remaining thyme, the tomato purée, garlic powder, onion salt, allspice, cinnamon, cloves, bay leaves, mustard seeds, brown sugar, apple cider vinegar, chilli flakes and a little salt and black pepper. Continue to cook for a couple of minutes and then leave to one side.

When the tomatoes are ready, add them to the pan and return to a low heat. Mix thoroughly and continue to cook for around a further 10 minutes, stirring occasionally. Remove the bay leaves and then leave the sauce to cool before transferring to a blender to blend until smooth. Pass through a strainer into a bowl and, once fully cool, transfer to an airtight container for storage in the fridge.

MAKES
ABOUT
700G/1½LB
V / WF / GF

kernels from 2 corn on the cob

1 small onion, chopped to around the size of a corn kernel

1 garlic clove, crushed

½ red pepper, chopped to around the size of a corn kernel

½ green pepper, chopped to around the size of a corn kernel

½ long red chilli, sliced

15g/½oz/4 tsp unrefined brown sugar

100ml/3½fl oz/scant ½ cup apple cider vinegar

100ml/3½fl oz/scant ½ cup water

1 tbsp olive oil

1 tsp mustard seeds

1 bay leaf

salt and black pepper

10g/⅓oz coriander (cilantro), finely chopped

1 x 700-ml/24-fl oz/3-cup jar, sterilized

SWEETCORN RELISH

Condiments are key to a top-of-the-range barbecue spread and this is one of our favourites; it works particularly well with veggie burgers or hot dog-type dishes. It's such an easy thing to make and lasts well in a sealed jar so is also ideal as a really special homemade gift.

Place the sweetcorn kernels, onion, garlic, red and green peppers, red chilli, brown sugar, apple cider vinegar, water, olive oil, mustard seeds, bay leaf and a generous pinch of salt and black pepper in a pan. Stir well as you bring it to the boil. Remove from the heat, add the coriander and then transfer to your sterilized jar.

Leave to cool, then seal with the lid and store in the fridge.

To sterilize your jar Bring a large pan of water to the boil. Remove from the heat and, using tongs, carefully lower the jar and lid into the water. Submerge the head of the tongs as well. Leave everything for 5 minutes then lift the jar out of the water using the same tongs and allow to air dry.

80g/2¾oz/⅓ cup tahini
½ garlic clove, crushed
1 tbsp lemon juice
3 tbsp water
pinch of salt

TAHINI SAUCE

This works with any Middle Eastern-style dish (we use it in our sabich, see page 56), but it is also excellent as a simple dip to enjoy with pitas or laffa and crudités. We also think it's great as a creamy vegan salad dressing.

Simply combine the tahini, garlic, lemon juice, water and salt in a bowl until well mixed and smooth.

ZHOUG

MAKES
ABOUT
150G/5½OZ
V / WF / GF

This Yemeni green chilli sauce is perfect whenever you want to add a herby kick to something, or a splash of the most gorgeous verdant green. It's delicious in our sabich (see page 56) and also with the shawarma-spiced celeriac (see page 69).

We've used green chillies as we're still in training on the chilli-eating front, but you could substitute for green finger chillies if you want to amp up the burn.

It keeps for a couple of days in the fridge but it's very quick to make and better eaten fresh.

Place the chillies, garlic, cardamom seeds, cumin and a dash of the olive oil into a blender and blitz until it starts to form a paste. Add in the parsley, coriander, mint, lemon juice, the rest of the olive oil, and a little salt and black pepper and slowly combine on low speed until fairly smooth. You can always add a splash of water if needed to blend.

3 green chillies, stalks removed and roughly chopped
3 garlic cloves
2 cardamom pods, seeds only
¼ tsp ground cumin
65ml/2fl oz/¼ cup olive oil
25g/1oz flat-leaf parsley, picked
25g/1oz coriander (cilantro), picked
10g/⅓oz mint, picked
juice of ½ lemon
salt and black pepper

HAY SALT

MAKES
ABOUT
20G/¾OZ
V / WF / GF

This ash salt certainly looks dramatic, yet it is such an easy thing to make and is very handy to have around to add a touch of the smoky great outdoors to any dish. It's best to do this in something cast iron, but at the very least make sure it's fireproof. The hay can be easily picked up at a pet shop but you can also experiment smoking with woods such as apple, oak or mesquite.

2 tbsp sea salt
3 handfuls hay

Place the hay in your Dutch oven and set the hay on fire. This is easiest using a blowtorch, if you have one. Allow the hay to burn completely to ashes and then transfer to a pestle and mortar along with the salt. Grind thoroughly and then push through a fine sieve (strainer). Store in an airtight container.

DRINKS

MAYAN-SPICED CAMPFIRE COCOA

2 tsp cocoa powder
600ml/21fl oz/generous 2½ cups whole milk
½ tsp ground cinnamon
pinch of cayenne pepper
4 drops orange extract, plus more to taste
2 tsp unrefined brown sugar, plus more to taste

Ideal for cold evenings around a roaring bonfire; a good hot chocolate is a sure-fire way to feel good about life. The zinginess of the orange extract coupled with the warmth of the cayenne and cinnamon in this cocoa is truly soul soothing.

Put the cocoa powder in a pan along with a few drops of the milk and mix to form a paste. Add the rest of the milk along with the cinnamon, cayenne, orange extract and sugar and slowly bring to the boil, stirring as needed. Sweeten further and add a little more orange if needed to taste.

Vegan option Use a milk alternative of your choice.

ROOIBOS & HONEY SWITCHEL

MAKES
2 LITRES/
70FL OZ
WF / GF

2 litres/70fl oz/8¾ cups water

3 rooibos teabags

50g/1¾oz fresh ginger, peeled and finely chopped

juice of 1 lemon, plus more to taste

4 tbsp apple cider vinegar (ideally organic and unfiltered)

6 tbsp honey, plus more to taste

1 x 2.5-litre/85-fl oz/10½-cup jar, sterilized

Switchel is a traditional woodsman's drink that's fast become one of our favourites – and it tastes all the better when enjoyed outdoors! Brilliant for restoring electrolytes, it's a great way of enjoying all the health benefits of unfiltered apple cider vinegar too. Rooibos is a super antioxidant tea and, as a South African, David always has a supply in the cupboard!

Bring the water to the boil, add the teabags, remove from the heat and allow to brew for about 5 minutes. Remove the teabags and leave the tea to cool.

Pour the tea into your sterilized jar, add the ginger, lemon juice, apple cider vinegar and honey, then seal and shake. You can enjoy it immediately over ice but it'll be even better if you transfer it to the fridge and leave it to brew for 12–24 hours.

Before drinking, you can add a little more lemon or honey to taste. We also like to keep the ginger in, but it can be strained out if preferred.

To sterilize your jar Bring a large pan of water to the boil. Remove from the heat and, using tongs, carefully lower the jar and lid into the water. Submerge the head of the tongs as well. Leave everything for 5 minutes then lift the jar out of the water using the same tongs and allow to air dry.

MAKES
1 LITRE/35FL OZ
V / WF / GF

200g/7oz fresh ginger, peeled and grated
80g/2¾oz/6 tbsp unrefined brown sugar
juice of 2 lemons
1 litre/35fl oz/4¼ cups sparkling water

EASY GINGER BEER

This easy-to-make ginger beer is so refreshing on a hot day. It's quite strong, which is how we like it (and it's great for blasting out a summer cold), but dilute with more water if you prefer. We hear it's also rather nice with a spot of rum.

Place the ginger in a bowl along with the sugar and lemon juice and muddle well. If you don't have a muddler, use a pestle or even a large stone.

Pour in the sparkling water, stir and set aside for 5 minutes.

Strain and then enjoy over ice.

NETTLE CORDIAL

MAKES
1 LITRE/35FL OZ
V / WF / GF

1 litre/35fl oz/4¼ cups water
25g/1oz dried nettles
100g/3½oz/½ cup unrefined brown sugar
4 thin slices lemon
still or sparkling water, to serve

This is a favourite spring-time sup and the flavour is a really unique one that's well worth trying. You can, of course, also use fresh nettles, which are easily found (just make sure you're wearing gloves to pick them), but we do tend to just use dried nettles to avoid the whole getting stung element! This is a great source of iron and has also been known to help with allergies, but for a bit more fun, it's also an interesting cordial to experiment with in cocktails.

Put the measured water and the nettles into a pan and bring to the boil. Remove from the heat, leave to steep for about 5 minutes (you want it to be very strong) and then strain into a bowl or jug. Discard the nettles (or use them to make a soup or pesto), then return the liquid to the pan. Add the sugar and return to the boil, stirring to fully dissolve all the sugar.

Add the lemon slices, then remove from the heat again, cover with a lid and leave out to infuse overnight.

Remove the lemon slices, transfer to a sterilized bottle (see page 115) and enjoy it over ice, diluted to taste with still or sparking water.

KVASS

375g/13oz bread of choice, ideally slightly
stale (but not a deal-breaker),
cut into chunks
2 tbsp dried peppermint
juice of ½ lemon
1.5 litres/52fl oz/6½ cups boiling water
30g/1oz/2½ tbsp unrefined brown sugar
pinch of salt
4g/⅛oz/generous 1 tsp easy bake yeast
5 raisins

This is a pretty out there concoction that will immediately transport you to
a wooden house in the forests of Siberia. It is not to everyone's taste but it's
a very interesting process and, being a ferment, it's full of probiotics to really
give you a boost. It's also a fabulous way of using up stale bread. This makes
quite a small amount so you can see if you like it before committing too
many resources!

Preheat the oven to 150°C/300°F/
Gas 2.

Place the bread chunks in a roasting
pan and toast them in the oven for
about 20 minutes until dried out.

Allow to cool, then transfer to a large
sterilized Kilner jar (see page 115) and
add the peppermint, lemon juice and
boiling water. Stir as best you can and
then seal and leave to one side on
the worktop overnight.

Pour the contents of the jar into a
large piece of muslin (cheesecloth)
placed over a bowl to strain out as
much liquid as you can. You will end

up with much less liquid than you
started with and this can be quite
slow going, but persevere and get as
much as possible. (We sometimes tie
the muslin onto our kitchen tap with a
bowl underneath and allow it to drip.)

Mix the sugar, salt and yeast into
the collected liquid, then return the
mix to the cleaned Kilner jar, seal
and leave on the worktop again to
ferment for 2–3 days.

Add the raisins, seal again and wait
(usually another day or two) for the
raisins to float to the top. The kvass is
then ready to drink and can be kept
for at least a few days in the fridge.

MASALA COFFEE

MAKES
2 CUPS
VO / WF / GF

There is little more pleasurable in life than a steaming hot cup of coffee after a night outdoors. Here, the addition of various spices makes it even more warming and soothing or it's also just a bit more special for an afternoon pick-me-up.

300ml/10fl oz/1¼ cups whole milk or milk of your choice

300ml/10fl oz/1¼ cups water

150ml/5fl oz/⅔ cup brewed coffee (we tend to use a percolator when camping)

½ tsp ground cinnamon

4 cardamom pods

¼ tsp ground ginger

pinch of grated nutmeg

1 tbsp unrefined brown sugar

Place the milk and water in a pot over your chosen heat source or on the hob and bring to the boil.

Add in the coffee and then the cinnamon, cardamom pods, ginger, nutmeg and sugar and bring back up to the boil.

Pour through a fine strainer into another pot and then briefly return to the heat whisking as you go to get it a bit frothy. Pour into cups and sweeten further to taste.

Vegan option Use a milk alternative of your choice.

MAKES
4 X 250ML/
9FL OZ
GLASSES
V / WF / GF

MINTY LEMONADE SLUSH

Known as 'limonana' in the Middle East, this super-refreshing drink is the perfect match for happy, sunny days outdoors. If you want to prepare it outdoors, you could make up the first stage at home and then buy some crushed ice to mix it with at the barbecue.

juice of 4 lemons

200ml/7fl oz/scant 1 cup water

70g/2½oz/5⅔ tbsp unrefined brown sugar, plus more to taste

10g/⅓oz mint, stems removed and leaves chopped, plus some extra sprigs for garnish

4 x 250-ml/9-fl oz glasses of ice

Put the lemon juice, water, sugar and mint into a blender and combine for about a minute.

Add the ice, blend on low to initially break it up and then increase the speed until you have a slush. Taste, add a little more sugar if you like it sweet, and then give it a quick final blitz.

Pour into glasses to enjoy immediately, garnished with a sprig of mint.

INDEX

SUPPLIERS

Big Green Egg
Can do it all, if you want a splurge.
www.biggreenegg.eu

Lodge
Cast iron heaven.
www.lodgemfg.com

London Log Company
A great place to source wood and charcoals for cooking
and also a great website for information on how to master
your fire.
www.londonlogcompany.blogspot.com

Netherton Foundry
For exquisite iron cookware.
www.netherton-foundry.co.uk

Sizzle Grills
Beautiful handmade fire pits, parrillas, chapas and more.
www.sizzlegrills.co.uk

Weber
Classic barbecues, plus accessories. We also really love their
'go-anywhere' range for when we're cooking on our little
terrace at home, or when we're camping or at the beach.
www.weber.com

THANK YOU

We're just so thankful to everyone at Pavilion for giving us the opportunity to write this book, one that has allowed us to indulge so many of our biggest passions. And to have a trilogy!

Thank you so much as always to Katie Cowan. And to Stephanie Milner – it's just been such a pleasure working with you and having the opportunity to get to know you. We also feel so honoured to have had our recipes graced once again by the design magic of Laura Russell, and a huge thank you as well to Claire Clewley for her work on the design and to Sarah Epton for copy editing. Thank you for everything, we're thrilled.

We were also so excited to have another chance to work with Liz and Max Haarala Hamilton, unquestionably the best food photographers around and just altogether brilliant people. Thanks are also due to Coco for expertly helping us to manage the cats vs. dogs situation with Jaffa!

We're also so grateful to Alex Gray for his food styling; it is such a pleasure cooking with you and generally just spending time with you and we can only aspire to your incredible levels of organization! As we can only aspire to the impeccable taste of the fantastic prop stylist Alexander Breeze – thank you so much for being involved again.

You're all such amazing, inspiring and talented people and we just wish we could always be writing recipe books so we could hang out with you all more often! We really hope we can have a reunion at the allotment (or perhaps Sri Lanka?!) sometime very soon.

On the subject of the allotment, we must also say a huge thank you to everyone at East Finchley Allotments. It is such a joy and privilege to live in London and have access to so much space for growing – we're so grateful for our plot and for all the work that's put into running the allotments so fantastically. We're also so grateful for their kindness in allowing us to shoot some of the photos for this book there.

We're forever grateful for the continued support of our families, our lovely doggy, Jaffa, and to all our wonderful Buddha Bowl customers who keep this whole shebang on the road.